MW00465431

**DONALD
SCHMIDT**

**A SEVEN SESSION
STUDY GUIDE**

Revelation

FOR
Progressive
Christians

WOOD LAKE

Editor: Michael Schwartzentruber
Proofreader: Dianne Greenslade
Designer: Robert MacDonald

Library and Archives Canada Cataloguing in Publication
Schmidt, Donald, 1959-, author
Revelation for progressive Christians : a seven session study guide /
Donald Schmidt.
Includes bibliographical references. Issued in print and electronic
formats.
ISBN 978-1-77343-150-5 (softcover).–ISBN 978-1-77343-151-2 (HTML)
1. Bible. Revelation–Commentaries. I. Title.
BS2825.53.S36 2018   228'.06   C2018-902534-4 C2018-902535-2

All scripture quotations arre from the Common English Bible,
copyright © 2011, Abingdon, Nashville, TN. Used by permission.

ISBN 978-1-77343-150-5

Published by Wood Lake Publishing Inc.
485 Beaver Lake Road, Kelowna, BC Canada V4V 1S5
www.woodlake.com | 250.766.2778

Wood Lake Publishing acknowledges the financial support of the
Government of Canada. Wood Lake also acknowledges the financial
support of the Province of British Columbia through the Book
Publishing Tax Credit.

Wood Lake Publishing acknowledges that we operate in the unceded
territory of the Syilx/Okanagan People, and we work to support
reconciliation and challenge the legacies of colonialism. The Syilx/
Okanagan territory is a diverse and beautiful landscape of deserts and
lakes, alpine forests and endangered grasslands. We honour the
ancestral stewardship of the Syilx/Okanagan People.

Printed in Canada. Printing 10 9 8 7 6 5 4 3 2

CONTENTS

FOREWORD

Amir Hussain

To begin with my own story: I came to the study of religion via the book of Revelation. In a course at the University of Toronto on William Blake, the visionary English poet and artist, Professor Jerry Bentley (of blessed memory) showed the class slides of Blake's "The Great Red Dragon and the Woman Clothed with the Sun." Blake had made two paintings with this title. One now resides at the National Gallery of Art in Washington, DC, and the other at the Brooklyn Museum. Professor Bentley told us that Blake's inspiration for this text was Revelation 12.

I put up my hand, and asked what that was. Professor Bentley began to recite the text, "There appeared a great wonder in heaven...," and I stopped him.

"No Professor Bentley, I mean, what's the book of Revelation?"

Professor Bentley described its place as the last book in the New Testament. I went home that night and began to read the New Testament for the first time. Not from the beginning, with the gospel of Matthew. Not from the end, with the start of the book of Revelation. But from the precise text that had inspired Blake – Revelation 12.

In hindsight, Revelation 12 was a great way to attract a young person with no interest in scripture to study the Bible. The words that begin the New Testament are in Matthew's gospel, where the author traces the genealogy of Jesus beginning with Abraham. It is, with no disrespect intended to Christians, not the most compelling text to bring in new readers. Revelation 12, by contrast, begins with a great hook. In heaven, a woman is pregnant, and a giant dragon, whose tail sweeps a full third of the stars out of the sky, is waiting to eat her child. All

of that action occurs in the first four lines of the chapter. I was hooked, even before I got to the seventh line in the chapter, about a war in heaven, where the dragon somehow has angelic helpers in his battle with the Archangel Michael.

Reading Revelation 12 got me interested in reading the whole book, which in turn inspired my interest in taking a course on the New Testament. From there, I did a Ph.D. in the study of religion, which led to my first job teaching at a university in Los Angeles. There, I met again the woman from the first line of Revelation 12, the "woman clothed with the sun, with the moon under her feet and a crown of twelve stars on her head," who is known as the Virgin of Guadalupe. All of this to state that the book of Revelation, introduced to me in a poetry course by the blessed Jerry Bentley, started me on my academic journey.

The book you hold in your hands, by the Rev. Donald Schmidt, may well begin you on your own journey. Many Christians are unfamiliar with the book of Revelation, something especially true for those who identify themselves as progressive Christians. Donald has done us a great service with this study guide for progressive Christians. It requires no background in the study of the New Testament, just a copy of the book of Revelation. It is a lovely book, both easy to use and easy to read, and it helps us to better understand the most misunderstood book in the Bible.

Amir Hussain, *a Canadian Muslim, is professor of theological studies at Loyola Marymount University, the Jesuit university in Los Angeles. The author of several books, including* Oil and Water: Two Faiths, One God (2006), *he is also an adherent member of Trinity-St. Paul's United Church in Toronto.*

HOW TO USE THIS BOOK

For group study

This book is primarily designed to be used in group settings, with minimal instruction for leaders. It is intended to encourage open conversation, for which this study guide is simply that – a guide. When your group gathers each week, you might want to spend a little time at the beginning of the session compiling a list of thoughts, comments, and questions that have arisen for people during the previous week, pertaining to their reading of Revelation. As a group, you can then try to address those questions and concerns during your conversation.

A good facilitator does *not* need to be a biblical scholar of any sort, just someone who can keep the session moving and the conversation on track. Leadership of the group could be held by one person or could change each time, but it is helpful to have a person in charge of the conversation so that the group does not get sidetracked or bogged down.

Spend time with the questions you'll find in the various boxes scattered throughout the text; they are designed to provoke reflection. If your group is large – perhaps with more than eight to ten people – you might want to divide into smaller groups to discuss the questions and to give people more time to share. But remember, whether you discuss the questions in the larger group or in smaller groups, there are no right or wrong answers. The goal is for group members to exchange thoughts, feelings, and opinions. No one has the definitive answer about what Revelation means, so the exchange of ideas should be your primary concern. It's okay for participants to disagree. The facilitator should try to hold people's differences of opinion carefully, and help participants respect each other's views.

The facilitator will want to look over the session ahead of time to get a sense of how much time to allot to the various questions and themes. The amount of time needed will depend on several factors, such as how many people are in the group, their familiarity with scripture, their theological stance, and so on.

For individual study

The best thing to do is simply to read the study, along with Revelation. I recommend reading Revelation from more than one version or translation, since this will allow you to compare translations. Mark the study guide up with interesting things you learn from other sources, or with questions. Spend time pondering the questions. You might wish to write answers in the margins, but it's far more important to simply let the questions guide your thinking and reflection.

In Lunenburg County, Nova Scotia, you will find Oak Island. I grew up hearing wonderful, fanciful stories of a treasure that had been buried on that island, and of how a complex system of tunnels enabled water to rush in, preventing anyone from gaining access to the treasure. According to the story, whenever anyone tried to dig down, the hole would fill up with water. Numerous attempts over the centuries to access the treasure had been doomed to failure.

Stories abound. Does Oak Island hold the treasure of Captain Kidd or of some other famous buccaneer? Some have speculated that artifacts from the Knights Templar are buried there, while others have claimed that Aztec treasure will someday be found at the bottom of the pit. The problem, however, is that so much digging has happened on Oak Island that there is no certainty – not even consensus – about where the original hole might be. The whole story is shrouded in mystery, and in doubt. So much so, that a reality TV show, *The Curse of Oak Island*, now in its fifth season, showcases the various theories and many attempts to find the treasure associated with the island. Of course, some say that Oak Island is simply a beautiful island, with nothing going for it except astonishing coastlines and gentle forests.

The book of Revelation is a bit like Oak Island. It is a powerful document that was written a long time ago to express a powerful message. Unfortunately, so many people have played with it, interpreted it, and found in it the things they *wanted* to find that it's a little difficult to "hear" the original text through all the noise of interpretation. Sometimes it seems like more material has been written about Revelation than about the rest of the Bible combined! What's more, people who write or talk about

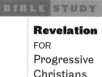

Revelation
FOR
Progressive
Christians

You Christians
look after a
document
containing
enough dyna-
mite to blow all
civilization to
pieces, turn the
world upside
down and bring
peace to a
battle-torn
planet. But you
treat it as
though it is
nothing more
than a piece of
literature.
– Mahatma
Gandhi

Revelation often do so with a passion that defies all logic. They speak vividly about plagues, and judgement, and the end of the world. All interesting themes – but are they as dominant as many of those people would have us believe?

The publication of this study came about because whenever I have led study groups on Revelation in progressive churches they have been well attended. People seem genuinely eager to know what this book is "really" about. When I led the study recently at my church in Kelowna, British Columbia, we anticipated about a dozen people, but over 30 showed up the first week.

One of the attendees quipped, "I wonder if there would be as many people here if Donald Trump hadn't been elected." We all laughed. But the comment says a lot about our general perception of Revelation. We have all heard stories about the end of the world, about some mythical beast or Antichrist with an odd number, about an abyss, and about some people being chosen while others are "left behind."

In this study, I invite you to think about the possible meanings of Revelation within the context in which it was written. In other words, what did it mean to the first people who read it? And what might it mean for us today?

When we set aside much of the nonsense and speculation from the last several decades, we find a story of God's presence with a fractured and frightened community, with a church that had no idea what the future might hold, and with a people who wondered if it was time to give up and abandon what they believed. Against this reality, Revelation assures these people that God will never abandon them. While it's true that a variety of dark images and themes exist in Revelation, the overarching message is about the presence of Christ (most often referred to as "the Lamb") as one who will heal the problems of the earth and its peoples, and who will offer a new age of inclusion. In other words, Revelation is *not* about the end of the world at some future date.

That being the case, it is possible to see Revelation as a fun, hope-filled book. It contains a lot of fanciful imagery and symbolic references, to be sure, but the bottom line is that it was written at a time when it was extremely difficult and dangerous to be a Christian. As such, it was meant to provide hope and encouragement to people who really needed it, and maybe it can still offer those things today, as well as challenge us to reflect on how we live *now*, as God's people.

A final thought. In this guide, you will always be encouraged to think for yourself. So don't be afraid of Revelation. Come with an open mind and an open heart, and listen to what God might be saying to you.

**The primary purpose of reading the Bible is not to know the Bible but to know God.
– James Merritt**

Disagreeing with the Bible

Everyone knows that David killed Goliath, right? After all, the story with all its gory details is presented in 1 Samuel 17. Except that 2 Samuel 21:19 tells us that Elhanan son of Jaare-oregim, the Bethlehemite, killed Goliath. Later still, in 1 Chronicles 20:5, we are told that Elhanan son of Jair killed Lahmi, the brother of Goliath. The point is simple; the Bible sometimes disagrees with itself. That's okay. We are allowed to disagree with the Bible, too. The goal is to find ways in which the biblical story can come alive for us, inform our daily living and, in all of that, bring us ever closer to God.

Introduction and Revelation 1

Introduction

Welcome to this study on the book of Revelation. It is subtitled "for those in progressive churches" because, sadly, the book of Revelation has largely been taken over by those in more conservative churches who see it as being filled with doomsday punishments for "bad guys," and predictions about how the world will end.

But I believe that is *not* what the book is about. Revelation was written as a letter around the year 95 CE by someone known as John of Patmos. (For the sake of ease, I will simply refer to him as John throughout this study.) We are not sure who he was, but we *do* know that it was difficult to be a Christian at that time in the Roman Empire, which was the only world John knew. Those in authority in Rome thought Christians were strange and they did not understand some of their odd behaviours, such as refusing to acknowledge the Roman emperor as Lord, and their bizarre practice of "cannibalism." After all, didn't they gather regularly to eat someone's flesh and drink their blood? Today we might smile at that kind of misunderstanding, but it was real in John's day.

> ■ What do you know about the book of Revelation?
> ■ What questions do you bring?
> ■ What hopes do you have?
> ■ What fears do you have?

John wanted to encourage the Christians he knew. He wanted them to realize that it was absolutely worth hanging on to their Christian faith and the values that Jesus taught and modelled, because, ultimately, what Jesus represented was far greater than all the power of Rome. This was an amazing statement given that Rome had huge armies and astounding dictatorial power, while Jesus was just a poor itinerant peasant who had wandered around Judea some 65 years earlier.

Yet think about it. Here we are reading John's book almost 2,000 years later. The Roman emperor and the Roman Empire are long gone, yet Christianity – in a vast array of forms – continues to flourish in many parts of the world. It seems John was right.

Another key theme in the book of Revelation is inclusion. John frequently speaks of people of all nations coming to know both Jesus Christ, and the God that Jesus made known. It is important to note that John does *not* say this to suggest that all people *must* someday acknowledge Jesus as Lord or be condemned to eternal punishment. Instead, John is excited to proclaim that everyone *can* come to know this loving God through Jesus Christ, and have a better life because of it. This is an important distinction. The whole world does not have to become Christian, but anyone – regardless of race, language, culture, status, etc. – *can* become a Christian. It is sad that so often this book – and the Bible as a whole – has been used to proclaim the opposite message.

What kind of book is Revelation?

Revelation is not a book of "facts." According to chapter 1, verse 10, it describes a vision, or a dream, that John had. Revelation tells about a dream or a vision, which means it is *not* telling us about things that have happened, or that are going to happen. Sometimes people read Revelation and get excited or worried about the things it says.

But just like the images we see in our own dreams, the images in Revelation are metaphor, and the text itself is written in a way somewhat akin to a political editorial today. In other words, Revelation was never meant to be taken literally.

Sometimes people think that taking a story metaphorically diminishes it, but that is not the case. Let's look at a quick example: Mark 4:35–41 *(see box)*. If we take this story literally, it has some intriguing benefit. For example, it tells us that should we happen to be in a boat on a lake, and Jesus is in the boat with us, and a storm comes up, Jesus can stop the storm and the boat will not capsize. That's good news, but it's very limited.

Mark 4:35–41

Later that day, when evening came, Jesus said to them, "Let's cross over to the other side of the lake." They left the crowd and took him in the boat just as he was. Other boats followed along.

Gale-force winds arose, and waves crashed against the boat so that the boat was swamped. But Jesus was in the rear of the boat, sleeping on a pillow. They woke him up and said, "Teacher, don't you care that we're drowning?"

He got up and gave orders to the wind, and he said to the lake, "Silence! Be still!" The wind settled down and there was a great calm. Jesus asked them, "Why are you frightened? Don't you have faith yet?"

Overcome with awe, they said to each other, "Who then is this? Even the wind and the sea obey him!"

On the other hand, if we take the story metaphorically, it tells us that whenever life becomes extremely difficult – as if we're in the midst of a storm and feel that there is no hope and that we're sinking – if we realize that Jesus is with us, we can probably get through it. For me, that's a much stronger meaning and message and it carries far more value for my day-to-day life. In other words, if we take the story metaphorically, it can apply to a far wider range of situations than if we take it literally, and it can have a stronger meaning for us.

As already mentioned, Revelation was written in the form of a letter, which makes it intriguing on a few fronts. First, letters are generally meant to be read all at once. That, of course, probably isn't practical for us when we read and study this book, but it is important to bear in mind. Each portion of the book, with a few exceptions, tends to build on what came before it. New sections will often begin with words like "and then" or "next," which are clues to how the writer was composing the text.

People who write letters also tend to make assumptions. If, for example, you were writing a letter to your aunt, you might talk about family members she knows. Perhaps you might write something like, "I hear Karen and Bob are going up to the old place again this year. I hope the others can go, too." Your aunt will undoubtedly know who Karen and Bob are, and she also probably knows who the "others" are and where the "old place" is that you refer to. But if someone else picked up the letter, they might not know. If they happened to know you or your aunt, they might be able to guess, and they may or may not be right. If someone completely unknown to the family or to you were to pick up the letter, there's very little they could know with any certainty.

That's a bit what reading Revelation is like; some parts are easy to figure out, but there are other parts that we can't know about for sure.

Who wrote Revelation?

The honest answer to that question is, "We don't know." The author is identified as "John," but that could mean anyone who bore that name, and it was a fairly common name. In Revelation 1:9–10, he speaks of being imprisoned on Patmos, an island off the coast of Turkey. *(See map below.)*

John is a prophet, of this we can be sure. But we need to remember that a biblical prophet is not someone who predicts the future. A prophet is someone who speaks of God's activity in the present. That's a huge and vital distinction. (The idea, presented in the gospel of Matthew, that Jesus was someone who fulfilled statements made by the prophet Isaiah has skewed our modern understanding of the word "prophet.")

This map shows the location of Patmos in relation to the seven churches to which John wrote the first part of the book of Revelation. The body of water in which Patmos is located is the Aegean Sea.

Patmos was not a penal colony, per se, but rather a heavily fortified island that the Romans often used as a place of banishment. Thus, when John explains that he is on the island "on account of the word of God," the implication is that he has been banished there for being a Christian, which is highly believable.

That's all we know about John from his self-descrip-

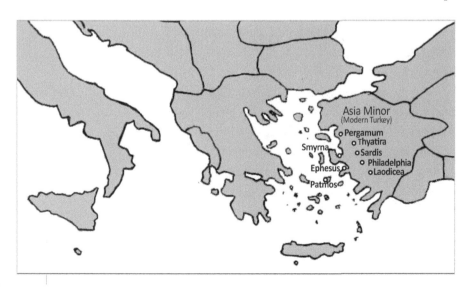

tion, other than the fact that he was writing around the year 95 CE, which eliminates anyone else by that name that we might know from the New Testament – for example, John the disciple and John the baptizer. As far as we can tell, John simply sees himself as a fellow Christian, stuck on an island with lots of time to think, and he has a wondrous vision of how God is involved in the life of our world.

Who was John writing to?

Revelation was written to a group of people who knew they had no power, and who therefore had very little hope. They had few choices available to them. In his book *Revelation: A Bible Commentary for Teaching and Preaching,* scholar Eugene Boring explains a little bit about how people in the early days viewed this odd little group.

Christians in Asia at the end of the first century had problems to face which the population at large did not. They were considered to be adherents of a sect that primarily appealed to the lower classes, a sect that had no long history or glorious institutions, a suspect group which met for its cultic practices in private homes on a day which was not a public holiday, a sect that was widely suspect of being unpatriotic, a group about which wild stories were told. After all, did they not speak of eating flesh and drinking blood (cannibalism!); did they not meet for private "love feasts" (incest! orgies!); had not their leader been crucified by the government as a rebel and enemy of the public welfare (unpatriotic!)?

To put it bluntly, people saw them as weird. It helps to remember that the Christian church, especially in the area where John was living and writing, was quite small, and that Christians were a minority within a minority (Judaism).

■ What might it mean that Revelation was written by someone who "shares with you in the hardship, kingdom, and endurance that we have in Jesus"?

The first recipients of the letter would have found in Revelation great encouragement. They would have been reminded that Jesus Christ was greater, and more worthy of love and devotion, than the Roman emperor or Rome itself. And they would have been reminded that, if they stayed true to their Christian faith, they would find a true reward in the end, whether the "end" meant life or death.

For what period in time was Revelation written?

Reading this book today with the assumption that it was written "there and then" about "here and now" is dangerous at best, and does not serve any useful purpose. That does not mean, of course, that the book is irrelevant for people today – far from it. But we have to be careful not to insert ourselves back into the biblical text.

Revelation 1:1 says that the things the book contains must "soon" take place. Clearly they did not take place in any literal sense of the word "soon." So was the author mistaken? Was the author deliberately misleading his readers? Or can we understand this book in a way that doesn't involve predicting the immediate future?

Much leads us toward an understanding of the book of Revelation that assumes it is telling us about the presence of God in the present, and about the promise of God to be with us always, even to the close of the age.

Who is God?

Before reading Revelation itself, we need to pause for a moment to contemplate who God is and what God is like – both for the author of Revelation and for us. We need not arrive at any final conclusions here, especially in terms of our own understandings, and it's worth pointing out that even John seems a little confused about this at times. But if we don't take time to do this, it will make our attempt to understand Revelation more difficult.

For the ancient people of Israel (of whom Christians are among the spiritual descendants) the key thing was that God is "One." There is no other God. There is only the one God, the God of Israel. This God is generally known by two names, and immediately confusion arises. One of the names is *Yahweh,* which is generally never pronounced by Jews and so in many English-language Bibles is rendered as LORD. The other name was *Elohim,* which is a little more complicated because the word is plural in Hebrew. Some scholars see this word as dating to a time when a belief in multiple gods was more common in the Ancient Near East. This latter name, *Elohim,* is sometimes shortened to *El* and in fact can appear as the suffix of various words – think of "Israel" (one who struggles with God) or "Emmanuel" (God with us).

It is helpful to have multiple names for the same God, because it helps us remember that there is no real way to define God, that all our definitions of God are finite and inadequate. Indeed, God is indefinable. Numerous words are used throughout scripture to describe God – father, mother, Lord, shepherd, servant, rock, gardener, and wind, to name only a few. All that is well and good.

But large numbers of people have one image that they hang on to tenaciously. These people see God as a "being," often anthropomorphic in nature, which is a fancy way of saying "like a human." Thus the ease with which we talk about God as a father or mother, or parent. In

part this is simply because it is difficult for us to imagine God as anything other than a "being" we can relate to. The only entity on the planet with which we can have conversation is another human being. Yes, we can talk to animals, and yell at our cars, and curse snow or rain, but actual back-and-forth conversation only really happens between humans. So we tend to view God in human terms and imagery, even if we readily admit that God is much, much more than that.

John was no different than us in this regard. His culture dictated various images of God, and he relies on some from scripture to support him. He is also influenced by the realities and expectations of his culture as he "fleshes out" his image of God.

■ **What are some of the images you have of God?**
■ **Which ones are your favourites?**
■ **Which ones bother you?**

The wrath of God

One of the cultural attitudes or beliefs we see reflected in Revelation has to do with the wrath of God. Several years ago, at a Christian educators' conference I attended in San Antonio, Texas, the speaker, John Holbert, invited the audience to turn to Psalm 137 in their Bibles. "If you want to know who the crazy person was who insisted we include all of this psalm in the current hymnal, it was me." People laughed. And then they read the psalm, in its entirety. It ends with the horrific words, "A blessing on the one who seizes your children and smashes them against the rock!" (Psalm 137:9)

This is a reminder to us that the Bible frequently speaks of the anger that all human beings feel from time to time. Sometimes we own that anger for ourselves, and sometimes we impose or project that anger onto God. We create God in our own image.

John sometimes does this too. Revelation sometimes – although not as often as some conservative Christians would have us believe – paints God as angry and wrathful. As progressive Christians, we tend to take a very dim view of this.

Hosea 11:4-9

I led them
    with bands of human kindness,
    with cords of love.
I treated them like those
    who lift infants to their cheeks;
    I bent down to them and fed them.
They will return to the land of Egypt,
    and Assyria will be their king,
    because they have refused to return to me.
The sword will strike wildly in their cities;
    it will consume the bars of their gates
    and will take everything because of their
    schemes.
My people are bent on turning away from
    me;
    and though they cry out to the Most High,
    he will not raise them up.
How can I give you up, Ephraim?
    How can I hand you over, Israel?
How can I make you like Admah?
    How can I treat you like Zeboiim?
My heart winces within me;
    my compassion grows warm and tender.
I won't act on the heat of my anger;
    I won't return to destroy Ephraim;
for I am God and not a human being,
    the holy one in your midst;
I won't come in harsh judgment.

While violent anger is shocking, disgusting, and hard to swallow for most of us – and when it is attributed to God we want to distance ourselves immediately – violent human anger is nonetheless real; and if we are honest we will probably be able to identify times when we have experienced our own feelings of this kind of anger, even if we've never acted upon them.

Here we need to remember that John and the people to whom he is writing are among the poorest of the poor. They live in a society and economic system that thrives on the exploitation of those at the bottom, and they are "it." The system is corrupt, mean, and their chances for advancement simply do not exist. Sometimes, as they look at the world around them, they get angry, and they imagine God must be angry, too.

Hosea 11 offers a wonderful glimpse of what can be seen as God's wrath, or anger. God laments over Israel and wishes they would return. "I led them with bands of human kindness...they are bent on turning away from me." And so at first God says, in essence, "Fine! Be that way! You want to go worship other gods, go and do it – get out of my sight!" But then God relents, and says "I can't give you up; I'm God, and not a human. I don't do that."

This piece is key and too often we forget it.

There's also another possibility to consider here. The plagues in chapter 6 can be read as depictions of God's anger, and often are. Yet they can also be seen as "natural consequences," which are different. One can look at the plagues, for example, and say they represent God's punishment of the world for being bad. Or one can read them as saying, "If you don't change the ways you are living, things will get worse."

In this era of climate change this is a key issue, because one can see climate change as a natural thing that cannot be helped, or as God's punishment for any number of things we may have done wrong (take your pick), or as something in between. We might, for example, see climate change as a natural consequence of our lifestyle, and we might choose to make changes to try and stop it.

When industrial pollution was seriously affecting major world cities in the 19th century, some called for regulations to stem the damage to waterways, air, and the general health and welfare of the population. However, such regulations would have cost money and, consequently, resulted in less profit. In response, many industrial giants decreed that to try to clean things up would be an insult to God, a way of saying that we did not trust God to take care of the world. Are the current results of such pollution divine punishment or natural consequence?

Many of us have no trouble with an image of God that includes anger at wrongdoing, though if we're honest we'll admit that we much prefer it to be aimed at others, and not at us. Still others prefer an image of God that does not include anger at all. What is key in many scriptural passages – and especially in the book of Revelation – is the recognition that a God who gets angry, even furious, nonetheless also offers forgiveness and hope – especially to those who are the most abused, neglected, and tossed aside.

■ How do you view the "wrath" or anger of God?
■ Do you believe God wreaks anger on those who disobey?
■ Is God always forgiving, or are there exceptions?

Chapter 1

Note: In anticipation of looking at the material in the first three chapters of the book, turn to "Numbers and Numerology" on p. 91. You may wish to keep a running list of the times various numbers appear, or at least make note of when they seem significant.

1:8 "**Alpha and Omega**" Alpha and Omega are the first and last letters of the Greek alphabet. Thus, Revelation 1:8 refers to God as "the beginning and the end." However, the first and last letters of the Hebrew alphabet (*aleph* and *taw*) were also sometimes used to refer to the *urim* and *thummim*, which were used by the ancient priests to determine God's presence with the people and to what the future held. Thus, describing God as the "Alpha and Omega" or "*aleph* and *taw*" could also be a way of saying "our destiny or future is in God's hands."

1:14–15 "**the Human One**" These descriptions of "the Human One" express incredible power:
■ eyes like a fiery flame (1:14) – implying that this is one who can see all things
■ feet like fine brass (1:15) – implying strength
■ a voice like rushing water (1:15) – implying that this is one who gives life or who offers a life-giving message

> ■ What might these images mean to us, that the Human One – whom we can assume here refers Jesus, although this is not always the case – can see all things, is strong, and offers life-giving words?

1:17–20 John is terrified of the vision he sees. However, Jesus reassures him and begins to explain what things mean. This, in turn, sets up the letters to the seven churches, which appear in the next two chapters.

■ Imagine that you are an early Christian reading this. What might it feel like to be told that God lasts forever? Or to be told that your destiny will be overseen or cared for by God?

A Closing Thought

The book of Revelation does not try to answer the questions "What will the end of the world be like?" or "When will the world end?" Rather, it seeks to answer the question, "Is God faithful?"

What do you think?

Revelation 2 – 3

Introduction

In this session, we focus primarily on several of the "letters" that were dictated within the book of Revelation. All of the letters are artificial – that is, they would not have been sent. Rather, they make statements about the various churches to whom they claim to have been written. As we read these letters, it can be helpful to wonder how they might apply to us – both to our churches and to other communities to which we might belong; as well as to ourselves as individuals. Let's look at each of the letters separately.

Why were these churches chosen?

Why were these churches chosen as the focus of these letters? The simple answer is that we don't really know. They may have been seven churches with which John was familiar, or they may be representative of issues he wished to raise. The fact that there are *seven* probably suggests the latter understanding – seven being a "perfect number" of churches modelling a "perfect set" of behaviours.

Each of the letters begins with the inscription "Write this to the angel of the church in..." This angel has no specific identity. Given that an angel is one who expresses God's message, we can assume that a church's angel is what we might also describe as its *essence,* the aspects of the church that define its character, and the message it proclaims on God's behalf. Thus, a letter to a church's angel is a letter that speaks directly to the heart of that congregation. As such, these are blunt letters that cut straight to the quick.

The ultimate measure of a man is not where he stands in moments of comfort and convenience, but where he stands at times of challenge and controversy.
– Martin Luther King, Jr.

Choices for Christians

There were few choices for Christians in the Roman Empire at the time this book was written. It's not that Christians were being killed on a regular basis, but they were certainly seen as second-class citizens, as we noted in the previous session. They were a small minority within another small minority (Judaism). They were misunderstood and, because of that, were generally despised. Why would anyone want to be a follower of Christ? Undoubtedly, many early Christians asked themselves this very question. The choices available to them were roughly these.

BIBLE STUDY

Revelation
FOR
Progressive
Christians

■ **They could quit.** It would not have been difficult to look around and conclude, "I didn't sign up for this; I'm out of here." Clearly some Christians would have made this choice, although we are not sure how many did that.

■ **They could lie.** We know that some Christians did this, too. They would practice Christianity in private, worship in secret, read specifically Christian materials only at home, and would not associate with other Christians in public. They could justify this by assuming that Jesus would understand.

■ **They could fight.** This was probably perceived by most people as being rather pointless, given the vast and very present might of the Roman army, and the fact that Rome had just crushed the Zealot rebellion – the "First Jewish-Roman War" that had taken place only a few decades before, from 66 CE to 73 CE. (There were two subsequent uprisings, from 115–117 CE and from 132–136 CE, which were also crushed by Rome.)

■ **They could try to change Roman law and practice.** This would have been an attempt to change public perceptions of Christianity. Some thought that if they could find a sympathetic Roman ear, they might be able to persuade that person or those people to convince others to "go easy" on the Christians.

■ **They could adjust to Roman oppression.** In other words, put up with everything. Don't intentionally make waves. If someone kicks you, or fires you from your job, or pushes your market stall over, let them.

■ **They could die.** This may sound awfully harsh to our modern ears, but it was John's preferred option. Remember: lifespans were relatively short in those days, especially for people who were in the lower classes, which was the case for most early Christians. Any number of things could kill you, so why not die for your faith? Proclaim your Christianity proudly and, should you be martyred for it, be glad.

> ■ Reflect on these various options. Which one(s) do you think you would risk? Why?

Chapter 2

A letter to the church in Ephesus

2:1 The one who holds the stars and lampstands (a perfect number of each) is the one who has things under control. (You may wish to locate these seven cities on the map on p.18.)

2:6 "Nicolaitans" We are not sure who the Nicolaitans were, but they are thought to have been promoters of an "accommodation theology" – that is, a theology that accommodated everyone, and stood for nothing.

■ It would appear that the church in Ephesus is trying to be all things to all people, which ends up leaving it somewhat devoid of principles. When has your faith been like this? When has your church been like this?

A letter to the church in Smyrna

2:9 "**I know your hardship and poverty, though you are actually rich.**" This sounds a bit like the Beatitudes; John recognizes that his readers may be poor in physical wealth, but he tells them that they are in fact very rich in faith, and very blessed by God.

2:9 "**...who say they are Jews (though they are not, but are really Satan's synagogue)**" Remember, Revelation is written for an audience that is essentially Jewish, or who at least see Christianity as a sect within Judaism. So this sentence is about those who claim to be faithful, but who in fact are backstabbing and mean-spirited in real life.

2:10 "**devil**" The term refers to an "accuser," more what we might define today as a "devil's advocate." This is not some odd creature wearing red and carrying a pitchfork, but refers to someone who, in the eyes of the author, opposes and challenges God at every turn.

■ What does it mean to you to "be faithful to the point of death, and I will give you the crown of life" (verse 10)?

2:11 "**second death**" This reference makes its only appearances in the Christian Bible in the book of Revelation. Although what the phrase meant to John seems pretty clear based on 21:8, many people have suggested alternative understandings.

> ### Different Christian views
> *(from Wikipedia.org)*
>
> **Although most Christians who believe in the immortality of the soul regard the second death to mean eternal suffering or torment in a place called the lake of fire, a few Christians believe in the immortality of the soul but teach universal salvation in which God will save everyone at some later time. Mortalists, including some Anglicans, some Lutherans, all Seventh-day Adventists, and others, oppose the idea of eternal suffering but believe that the second death is an actual second death and that the soul perishes and will be annihilated after the final judgment.**
> *– https://en.wikipedia.org/wiki/Second_death; accessed August 15, 2017*

A letter to the church in Pergamum

2:13 "Satan's throne" Pergamum, which John refers to as "Satan's throne," was actually a very large city of some 200,000 inhabitants. The cityscape was dominated by a huge temple built to honour the Egyptian gods Isis and/or Serapis. In the year 92 CE, the first Christian bishop of Pergamum was murdered in the temple after a class with worshippers there.

2:17 "White stone with a new name" White stones, when cast by those voting on a jury, meant that the accused would live; a black stone meant they would die.

Often when people recovered from a serious illness, they were given a new name, as if they had essentially died and been reborn. Thus, this verse is about God offering a second chance.

> ■ **The letter to Pergamum is about second chances. When have you felt like you have been given a second chance?**

A letter to the church in Thyatira

A problem with life in Thyatira came from within the church. As a thriving commercial city, Thyatira had many trade guilds and the church encouraged people to be a part of them. These guilds often had wild dinners that included a lot of drinking, and "relaxed sexual practices," as one commentary nicely put it. In writing this letter, John challenges such behaviour, suggesting that the church should be above all of that.

2:20 "That woman, Jezebel" This refers to someone who was leading the people astray, in a manner similar to the Jezebel who supported false prophets in the time of Elijah. The sexual immorality referred to is the act of sleeping with non-Christians.

2:22 The original of this verse implies that "she" and her consorts are being tossed onto a bed where they will fornicate themselves into oblivion; it appears early biblical copyists and translators were uncomfortable with the verse, since it has been altered and corrupted in many ancient manuscripts.

■ The situation in Thyatira begs a larger question: is an active church always a healthy church? Think of your own faith community and of others with which you are familiar. In some cases, people come to be entertained rather than instructed, or to be soothed instead of encouraged to challenge injustice. What does it mean to be a healthy church? What does it mean to be a success-ful church?

Chapter 3

A letter to the church in Sardis

According to the writer, the church in Sardis is wishy-washy. They were proud never to have had any heresies or disagreements. Yet sometimes the church is called to take a stand, even when doing so can be controversial. "A truly vital church is always under attack," says William Barclay in his commentary on *Revelation* (Vol. 1, p. 118). Or to quote one of the characters from the TV show *The West Wing*, "When they're shooting at you, you must be doing something right."

3:1 **"you are in fact dead"** The word dead here is a euphemism for "untrue" or "dishonest."

3:4 **"Who haven't stained their clothing"** This is an interesting phrase and can be taken more than one way. Literally it means those who have not messed their pants, to be polite about it. To go to the bathroom in one's clothing is to render oneself unclean. Beyond the literal meaning, however, it possibly refers to the *actions* of those in Sardis, which John criticizes in verse 2: "I've found that your works are far from complete in the eyes of my God."

Thus they are "unclean." But the reference to those who haven't stained their clothing also suggests impatience and a lack of social graces. Thus, the phrase could refer to those who have shown their impatience by "soiling" themselves instead of waiting for Christ's arrival.

3:5 The Romans kept lists of citizens and could blot anyone's name off it for serious misbehaviour. Sardis' claim to fame was that it was known for its work with wool; it is the first place where wool was dyed with artificial dyes as a major commercial enterprise. Thus, the statements about wearing white clothing probably imply that God will dress us in clothing that is pure, simple, straightforward – not overdone with bright colours for show.

■ Does your faith community embrace or shy away from controversy? What do you think of churches that are always under attack? What do you think of churches that are never under attack?

A letter to the church in Philadelphia

3:7 "key of David" This phrase implies access to the temple, which means access to God.

3:12 "I will make them pillars in the temple of my God." A temple is the place where we worship God, and it is the place where we can most closely encounter God's presence. Thus, to be a pillar in the temple is to be one who holds up a place where people can come to connect with God.

■ How is church a place where we encounter God? What makes it so for you?

A letter to the church in Laodicea

3:14 "Amen" is the "last word" or the "Right on!" of God.

3:16 **"Because you are lukewarm, and neither hot nor cold, I'm about to spit you out of my mouth."** This is a common theme and a complaint John holds against many of the churches. Here it is stated most bluntly. Christ does not like it when we do not stand for something. Or as we often hear people put it today, "If you don't stand for something, you'll fall for anything."

3:17 "you are miserable, pathetic, poor, blind, and naked" Laodicea was such a wealthy community they turned down government assistance after an earthquake struck in 17 CE. For a place that thought it had it all, it must have been devastating to be told that, in fact, they had nothing. John challenges them to seek their wealth not from the world, which has served them very well, but from Christ.

As I am writing this, a news story is brewing in the United States regarding a riot in Charlottesville, Virginia. The riot began when a group of white supremacists, who had a permit to hold a rally, were confronted by a group of counterprotesters. In the ensuing struggles, three people were killed and several injured.

What is intriguing about the story is that many people were quick to condemn the white supremacists, going so far as to claim they were terrorists. However, U.S. President Donald Trump would not do so, instead insisting that there was violence on both sides, and that no one was more to blame than anyone else.

■ How does one choose who is right?
■ How does one choose which stand to take?
■ What might be the consequences?

Closing Thoughts

Some people expect Christians to be perfect and to always live up to the ideals of Christ. Other people have been asked to leave churches and have been told they are not welcome because of who they are, how they dress, ideas they hold, and so on. Within denominations, congregations can embody an incredibly wide range of views on "acceptable" behaviour. (The range of views within any given congregation can also be incredibly wide.)

How do you discern what is "the right church" for you? When you find the "right" church, does that mean the others churches are wrong, or just different?

■ ■ ■

Reflect on these letters for a while. Individually or in a small group, try writing a letter to your church in this style. Discuss these letters. You could also share them with the minister and/or the governing bodies in your church. After you have finished this study, reread your letter. Has your perspective changed? Has anything within your church changed?

■ Which was your favourite letter? Why?
■ If John were writing such a letter to your church, what might he say?
■ Several scholars note that differences in the language used in these chapters suggest that they may have originated from a different source or a different time. Does that matter to you? How might that possibility change your understanding of the book as whole?

Revelation 4 - 8:1

In this session we shift gears and begin to encounter some of the visions that John had. The letters contained in chapters 2 and 3 are of a different style – so much so that some scholars believe they come from a different source, or that at least were not initially part of the book of Revelation. Thus, many see chapter 4 as a direct continuation from chapter 1.

John's visions are wild and beautiful. We need to remember that this is a dream, and as such it contains the

I came to poetry through the urgent need to denounce injustice, exploitation, humiliation. I know that's not enough to change the world. But to remain silent would have been a kind of intolerable complicity.
– Tahar Ben Jelloun

God's throne

About 75% of the references to thrones in the Bible come in the book of Revelation. The image of God – or of Jesus, referred to as "The Lamb" – sitting on a throne is in direct contrast to the image of Caesar sitting on the throne. John's point is clear; God's power is greater and longer-lasting than Caesar's. Rome's power may seem to be impenetrable, but it is not.

The use of the word "throne" is therefore very political and carries great power. Imagine you are a part of the early church; you are poor; you have very little hope; you are laughed at, spat upon, and told you belong to a weird sect. On a daily basis people challenge you to give up this silliness and join the majority – in other words, accept the authority of Rome and abandon Christianity. Over and against this, John provides countless images of God sitting on a throne. Suddenly, you feel empowered. Maybe there is a reason to remain a Christian after all.

kind of imagery common to dreams. Like a cartoon, natural laws of physics do not need to apply here. As with a good fantasy novel, we are encouraged to stretch our imaginations and in so doing learn much about things that are true, even if they are not factual.

Chapter 4

4:3 "jasper, carnelian, emerald" Each of the ancient 12 tribes of Israel had a gemstone, rather like birthstones in other traditions. Jasper was the stone for Benjamin, the youngest; carnelian for Reuben, the eldest; and emerald for Judah, the strongest. Thus it seems the one seated on the throne holds the power of all the tribes of Israel. The people reading this would probably have known of the stones, as they were a part of this tradition.

4:4 "twenty-four" Note the symbolism of the number 12 and that it is doubled here. This presumably refers to the 12 tribes of Israel plus the 12 disciples – seen by many as the "new" Israel. Thus, this group can be seen as a blending of old and new, or as being twice as strong/ important/powerful.

4:5, 7 Note the use of the numbers seven and four in these verses. Both of these numbers are significant. (See "Numbers and Numerology" on p. 91.)

4:7 There are four living creatures listed here. Tradition has ascribed each of them to one of the gospel writers, although this is a later interpretation. The original idea may have been that they represent all of creation:
■ the noblest *(lion),* or wild animals
■ the strongest *(ox),* or domestic animals
■ the wisest *(human)*
■ the swiftest *(eagle),* or birds

This list is based on the general ancient assumption that insects and reptiles did not count (they were seen as cursed), and that sea creatures did not count either (they were not seen as being in the same category as other animals because they did not appear to breathe air).

4:8 "**six wings...and each was covered all around and on the inside with eyes**" The six wings give great speed. Having eyes all around means a) they can see everything, and b) they can readily see into people's souls, for these were seen as the two purposes of the eye.

4:11 This short hymn would have been highly significant to the people who first read this book. To say that God is worthy is to imply in the same breath that Caesar is *not* worthy. In addition, the statement, "It is by your will that they existed and were created" suggests that all of creation is here because God wants it to be here. This would have been very good news to a people who otherwise felt unworthy, or who were told on a regular basis that they should disappear.

> ■ **What does it feel like to be told that you exist by God's will?**
> ■ **When you are mocked for your beliefs, what does it feel like to recognize that God is more powerful than the seeming powers of the world?**

Think of groups today who are told essentially the same thing – that they should disappear. Obviously, the groups you name will vary depending on where you live and what is going on in the world. At various times throughout history, Jews, Muslims, women, gays and lesbians, and others have found themselves facing such attitudes. Imagine yourself as a member of a group that is looked down upon. If you're a member of such a "group," what does it feel like?

Chapter 5

5:1 "scroll" Whenever we see the word "scroll," it helps to remember that it simply refers to a document or a book. Scrolls were simply the form documents took in ancient times. Scrolls were sealed with wax, which was essentially the equivalent to signing one's signature. If the seal was broken, it was assumed that the document had been opened and presumably read. Notice that this document is sealed seven times – a perfect number, suggesting it is a special document.

The Lamb

John frequently portrays Jesus as a lamb in Revelation. Interestingly, a lamb is an unusual choice to indicate power and authority, which are also ascribed regularly to Jesus in this book. The contrast is quite intentional and is used as a way of saying that things that appear weak (a lamb is, after all, a rather helpless animal) can sometimes surprise us. Such is the case with Jesus. He is referred to in Revelation 5:6 with a diminutive term, translated as "lamb," but more accurately perhaps as "lambi-kins." It's as if John is having a bit of fun with this image and making a profound point at the same time: "Jesus may seem to be powerless, like a lamb, yet he has seven horns [complete or perfect power] and seven eyes [complete or perfect wisdom]." In other words, this lamb, which even appears dead in some parts of the vision, still has more power than Rome. Such is the amazing power of God!

5:5 "Lion of the tribe of Judah, the Root of David" These are symbolic names or titles, thought to refer to any person in the lineage of David. Interestingly, there were lions in Palestine in biblical times. They are thought to have gone extinct in that area sometime between the 16th and 19th centuries.

5:7–8 Jesus comes, takes the scroll, and the four living creatures (all of creation) and the 24 elders (the 12 tribes of Israel plus the 12 disciples – the "new" Israel) fall down before the lamb, recognizing his worth.

Substitutionary atonement

Conversation about the Lamb of God can readily bring up the idea of "substitutionary atonement," which has been a doctrine in various circles of the church since New Testament times. In a nutshell, this is the concept that humanity has sinned so badly that God required a sacrifice to "atone" for our misdeeds, to bring us back into right relationship with God. This sacrifice was, of course, understood as Jesus.

Those who agree with this doctrine point to key texts such as Isaiah 53, which is usually read on Good Friday, thus reaffirming the concept. Isaiah, of course, was written long before Jesus, and thus requires us to understand it as predicting him for it to apply cleanly. Other texts include Matthew 8:16–18 , where Matthew quotes Isaiah to say that Jesus "is the one who took our illnesses and carried away our diseases"; and Romans 5:11, where Paul writes that we can take pride in Christ "through whom we now have a restored relationship with God."

Those who question this doctrine note that texts such as these can also be understood in other ways – Jesus can take away illness and

■ When have you seen images of Jesus portrayed as a lamb? Does that connote weakness or power for you?

5:9 "You are worthy" The implication is that Jesus is worthy, and by extension no one else is.

5:11, 13 All manner of creatures, including "thousands of thousands" of angels(!), recognize the power of Jesus.

disease and restore our relationship with God without needing to be seen as a sacrifice. Further, some point out that this doctrine requires us to accept that, while the prophets (claiming to speak on God's behalf) frequently denounced the sacrificial cult in no uncertain terms, God has rather arbitrarily restored it.

While John certainly would have had access to Isaiah, we cannot know if he would have had access to any of the written New Testament texts. It's possible, but we have no way of knowing. Paul's letters precede Revelation, but were addressed to specific churches and may not have been widely circulated at John's time, and the gospels are often understood as being roughly contemporaneous with Revelation.

Given that the doctrine of substitutionary atonement has often been used by church authorities to control people and make them subservient, many approach it with caution. Whether *John* intended it here is, I believe, doubtful, although not outside the realm of possibility.

For more on this, you may wish to explore the writings of Marcus Borg, specifically *The Heart of Christianity* (p. 95).

As if that wasn't enough, every creature "in heaven and on earth and under the earth and in the sea" does as well. This is a powerful statement because, as mentioned before, creatures that lived under the earth (thought to be the home of all reptiles and insects) and in the sea were thought to be cursed, or not as good as other animals. Yet even these creatures recognize and praise the glory of God.

> ■ **How does creation worship God?**
> ■ **What does it mean that all kinds of creatures worship God and recognize God's authority?**

Chapter 6

Horses were war animals, and for the Jews they were a foreign animal. Thus, horses were "exotic," and seem to portend bad things to come. The description of those bad things should not be taken literally, however. Remember – this is a vision! The message – through all the details of the opened seals, wild horses, and other things – is that life is going to take a turn for the worse for a while (an understatement if there ever was one!), but that Christians are called and challenged to hang in there.

6:2 The white horse seems to represent physical strength.

6:4 The reference to a red horse signifies bloodshed and death. This was not an uncommon symbol at that time.

6:6 The black horse symbolizes inflation, which would have had a devastating effect on the Christians, who were generally already cash-strapped.

Inflation – it's not new!

A modern example of hyperinflation occurred in the Weimar Republic in Germany between the First and Second World Wars. In 1918, one paper Deutschmark (DM) was equal to one gold mark; by 1923, it took 1,000,000,000,000 (one trillion) paper Deutschmarks to equal one gold one. To put it in another perspective, it took 4,210,500,000,000 (4 trillion, 210 billion, 500 million) Deutschmarks to purchase one U.S. dollar.

John – and many others of his time – believed that the inflation they were experiencing had been created by an unjust economic system and could thus have been avoided. We know too well that the inflation of the Weimar Republic – and the financial ruin it brought to the vast majority of Germans – contributed to the popularity and rise of the Nazi party. Desperate times often create yearnings for desperate solutions. This was no different in the era of the early church.

6:8 The pale green horse appears to symbolize sickness, which would be in keeping with the rest of John's writing. Early Christians, again because they tended to be poorer, were at higher risk of the perils caused by famine and pestilence, which were hardly uncommon in those days.

■ The image of the "four horses of the apocalypse" has been used in a variety of ways. It would appear, however, that they are merely devices for John to indicate that things are going to get worse before they get better. What are some other historical examples of this?

6:9–11 This section speaks about early Christian martyrdom, which was shifting in its popularity at the time Revelation was written. Earlier Christians had been strong supporters of martyrdom (that is, of dying for the faith) because, if Jesus was returning soon, what did it matter? As more and more time passed and the return of Jesus seemed to be delayed, the desire for martyrdom began to wane. John, on the other hand, seems to suggest that, if for no other reason, at least suffering for our faith is admirable. The notion of avoiding suffering is a fairly modern one. Its popularity in some circles of Christianity stems from the Western idea that we can overcome all the powers of the universe. For John, this was unheard of and unimaginable.

6:12–17 The image here clearly is one of the leaders of the world desperately trying to hang on to power, with disastrous results. As elsewhere, John's key point is to tell us that, ultimately, Christianity will triumph over all other forces in the world.

Chapter 7

It is good to move quickly from chapter 6 to chapter 7 because the break is quite arbitrary and the two pieces flow together. After the vision of the disasters, John presents an image of four angels standing in the four corners of the earth; people thought the earth was flat, so it would literally have four corners. Four is also an image of completeness, of balance, and, in the midst of this, comes a calming word.

7:3 To put a seal on something was to claim it, to identify it. In the days before identity cards, some kind of physical mark (a brand, a tattoo, circumcision, or manipulation of some body part such as a lip or ear) was the best way to identify people, and to show who belonged to which group.

The caution not to damage anything until a seal has been placed on all those who serve our God suggests both a protective measure, and also the possibility that Christ has a desire to postpone the end of things.

7:4–8 **"one hundred forty-four thousand"** This number has caused all sorts of speculation, but it's not as difficult to understand as some have tried to make it. Think of the 12 tribes of ancient Israel, multiply them by the 12 tribes of the "new" Israel (an image the church often used for the 12 disciples of Jesus), and then multiply that by a "great big number," or infinity, which was pretty much how people understood a "thousand" in ancient Israel. What you get is a huge, infinite number that seems to represent ancient Israel writ large. As if to emphasize this, the 12 tribes are now listed, one by one.

7:9–17 What follows is a rather familiar passage. (It appears in the *Revised Common Lectionary*, and is sometimes read at funerals.) It indicates that in the midst of all this destruction and devastation, a number of people will survive. They have washed their robes in blood, but those robes have turned to white. Taken literally, it makes no sense. But the author's concern here is symbolism, and it has that clearly. John wants us to believe that when we submit to the Lamb, who has died, and commit ourselves

to the direction in which he seeks to lead us, the forces of the earth have no power over us. In other words, we can survive, and carry on, often stronger than we were to begin with.

> ■ The image of the "church triumphant" presented in verse 9 is worth noting. What kind of people are part of this community?
> ■ What does this say about who is included in the community of God's people?
> ■ How does this sit with common interpretations of Revelation?

8:1 The opening of the seventh seal is almost anticlimactic. Nothing happens. There is a moment of silence. It is as if the thing that mattered was *not* the devastation that was spoken of, but the survival of those who will give themselves to the Lamb (Jesus).

Closing Thoughts

In chapter 5, a great deal of emphasis is placed on the fact that all of creation is worshipping God and the Lamb (Jesus, the Christ). We need to be careful, however, not to assume this means that everyone will become a Christian, which is an interpretation often imposed on the text. This can certainly be one interpretation, but it does not necessarily mean that *all* people need to become Christian. This is an important question today, when we seek to recognize the validity and value of other forms of religious and spiritual expression.

How important is it to you to think of all the peoples of the world someday becoming Christian?

Revelation 8:2 – 11

In this session we explore several more chapters depicting similar plagues, before shifting gears with Revelation 12. One can see the plagues as "doom and gloom," but there really is much more here – particularly a concern for justice, and a concern for creation.

Chapter 8

Read again "Numbers and Numerology" on p. 91, specifically the information about the numbers 3, 4, and 7. All three numbers will come to play in this chapter and following.

8:2 Angels are simply messengers from God.

8:3 Incense was burned to please God. The idea was that people could burn sacrifices to appease God, and that God (who was thought to dwell in the sky) would smell the smoke as it wafted upward. Adding incense made the smell more attractive, and thus would please God more. Over time, incense became associated with drawing God's attention to our prayers.

8:5 The angel tosses down the burning incense, as if to suggest that either the angel or God is angered or frustrated with humankind. Our prayers are not worthy of God's attention, and thus incense is of no use.

8:6–13 This passage is strongly symbolic and depicts the natural world being disgusted with the affairs of humanity. Of course, the human affairs with which the natural world is disgusted would be those of the non-Christian

> Too many people find no meaning in life. They have closed their hearts to the mystery. Don't they know that the bread of life is baked for them too, not just the earthly bread? All they have to do is ask.
> – Barbara Gibson

powers. Notice how a third of the trees, the sea, the rivers, and other things disappear. Remember again the significance of the number three – it indicates balance, because a three-legged stool or chair or table cannot wobble. However, if you take away a third of that, it falls over. Enough of the natural world is sufficiently angry that all balance in the universe seems to be thrown out of kilter. This is in direct contrast to the images of natural balance presented in the creation story in Genesis 1. (See also the box "The wrath of God" on p. 22.)

8:8 The reference to a mountain burning with fire and being cast into the sea could refer to an actual volcano. (We know that various volcanos did indeed erupt in the greater Mediterranean area around the time this book was written.) However, it could also refer to a general hope or imagining – Babylon (which is really just a reference to Rome) was pictured as being on a mountain, and so there was always the hope that it would be cast into the sea.

Revelation 8:6–13 is a scathing commentary on the state of the world. It is a reminder that environmental devastation is not a new phenomenon, but has been going on for a long, long time. Some would see this as a reassurance: people have always been destroying the environment, and it continues on, so issues like climate change and pollution don't matter. Others would say, "We have been doing this for a long time, and we need to stop or the end – as predicted in Revelation – will indeed come." ■ What do you think? Why? How does the environment indicate to us that it is fed up or angry with our behaviour?

8:11 "Wormwood" This word was at times used to refer to injustice. It was also used as a nickname for the king of Babylon and thus, by extension, would be a thinly-veiled reference to the Roman emperor. (See "Babylon, Rome, and Parthia" on p. 94.) Other synonyms for the ruler of Babylon were Lucifer (light), Daystar, and Offspring of the Dawn – all of which were titles indicating someone who was trying to take over from God, or to play God. This would have been of great concern for John, who clearly believed that no one should do that.

8:13 Curiously, in the United States, the image here of an eagle flying overhead has been interpreted as a symbol of the United States. Some have gone a step further and have suggested that this indicates the U.S. flying over the world and passing judgement.

To think that scripture written some 1,900 or so years ago would predict a nation of the modern era is both naïve and dangerous. In ancient Rome and Israel, the eagle was recognized as one of the greatest and strongest of all creatures – and thus, most able to survive. It is not a surprise that it would fly over the devastation and be horrified. Presumably with great sadness, the eagle pronounces that things will get worse.

Chapter 9
9:1–5 Life will indeed not be good for a while, to put things mildly. A huge abyss will open up, with smoke rising from it. This is one source of current notions of hell as a place of eternal fire under the earth. This has led to many misunderstandings – exacerbated by the fact that some translations make a distinction between the abyss in chapter 9, and the "lake of fire" in chapter 20, and this in turn is supported by variations in manuscripts. These variations could suggest that early readers had difficulty with the place and thus felt a need to change the text, or

they could simply be first-century "typos." In other words, whether the lake of fire or the burning lake to which some evil people are confined later in the book are the same thing as the abyss or something different is unclear.

The significance of the abyss is that, in 20:3, the dragon, described as "that old snake" and "the satan," is confined to it for 1,000 years.

9:6 There is true sadness in this verse; the suffering will be so great people will want to die, but will not be able to. From this perspective of utter pain and hopelessness,

---

The Beatles and Revelation 9

For many people, Revelation 9 conjures up images of Charles Manson and The Beatles. Charles Manson lived in California in the late 1960s, and preyed on women and men who felt alone, abandoned, or rejected. As he espoused his philosophy, they fell under his spell and would do anything for him. This was proven when, on two consecutive nights in August of 1969, he sent groups out to commit murder, leaving seven innocent people dead.

What is more intriguing is that Manson based his reason for the killings on his interpretation on Revelation. Specifically, he believed (or claimed to believe) that the Beatles were the four angels of the apocalypse described in chapter 9 and that they had inspired him to begin a revolt of Black people, which would result ultimately in Whites conquering them. It was a bizarre idea (to say the least) and pathological. In particular, Manson focused on verses 7–10 as describing The Beatles:

■ human faces and women's hair (The Beatles "introduced" long hair)

death itself comes to represent "hope," because it repre-sents release.

9:13–19 Rome was terrified of the Parthians, who lived beyond the Euphrates. (See the article "Babylon, Rome, and Parthia" on p. 94.) This paranoia and fear is akin to what many Germans felt towards the Jews, and to what many Westerners feel towards Muslims. In both modern cases, this fear and paranoia began with a few isolated incidents that had nothing to do with the people being either Jewish or Muslim. Over time the paranoia grew to

■ iron armour upon their chests (electric guitars)
■ sound of their wings was loud (amplified music)
■ tails with stingers (electrical cords)

There was also to be a king whose name, in Latin, was Exterminans; Manson saw himself as that king. He referred to the race war that he would start as "helter skelter" which was the name of a Beatles song. Manson also believed that he would lead his followers into the "great abyss" under the earth to wait out the pending race war. In the United Kingdom, the term "helter skelter" refers to a piece of playground equipment; in North America we would call it a slide.

■ What do you make of the irrational fears that nations have of others – or that individuals such as Charles Manson seem to have of others?
■ What examples are you aware of where such fear has led to dangerous or disastrous actions? What can be done to counter such fear?

pharmakon and *porneia*

Two words in Revelation 9:21 bear a closer look. *Pharmakon,* generally translated as "potions," took on the sense of charms or magic, and thus was often used as a term indicating sorcery. It referred literally to any substance that would change the nature of the one who partook of it. The word is, in fact, the source of our words "pharmacy" and "pharmaceuticals." Scholars are divided as to whether it refers to witchcraft or sorcery, or if it is confined to potions and consuming strange things, or even if it should be connected to the word that follows it, and thus refer to "contraceptive potions." Such things were not unheard of in those times, and in theory enabled one to participate more freely in sex without concern for unwanted pregnancy. Even if this last meaning is the correct one, it should not be seen as a condemnation of contraception in the modern world; it would have

a dangerously irrational level.

In this part of the dream or vision, it is the Parthians who are seen to be coming, riding horses that are quite horrendous to behold. And there seem to be millions of them!

9:20–21 These verses tell us that those who weren't killed because of their evil nevertheless refused to repent. In other words, in John's vision, there are no good people in the world – none. Everyone seems committed to ignoring God and God's call to live lives of justice and righteousness.

been intended here solely in the context of the next word, *porneia.*

Porneia is usually translated as "sexual immorality." It is a vague term, and so we need to be careful with it, because few things can get people more excited than rulings on sexual matters, especially when they are found in the Bible. The immorality referred to here was the wanton sleeping around often done by non-Jews and non-Christians, frequently in the name of their religion or as part of a religious rite. Both Jews and Christians considered such sexual practices to be wrong. This condemnation may stem from (or be the source of) the ancient Hebrew belief that not obeying the God of Israel was comparable to sleeping around with other gods. Adultery and idolatry were often seen as one and the same. Later manuscripts tended to replace this word with *poneros* which means "wickedness."

■ Think for a moment of the many times people grab hold of an isolated phrase in scripture and make it bigger, using it to formulate policies and rules. Why do you think that happens?

Chapter 10

10:1 "rainbow" The rainbow was seen as a symbol of hope. In Genesis, God places a rainbow in the sky as a reminder and a promise or covenant that never again would God destroy the earth with a flood, or anything else. It is important to keep the rainbow in mind as a backdrop for the plagues.

10:2 "open scroll" This could also be read as "little scroll," which would be the same as saying "booklet" today. Thus, it refers to a short message.

■ Frequently the message in Revelation broadens to include a diverse range of people. Why do you think that is?
■ Do you think the diverse range of people is meant to include only the people who are named (after all, why name some people if you also include others) or is it meant to symbolize a wider diversity?

10:9 "Take it and eat it. It will make you sick to your stomach, but sweet as honey in your mouth." The prophetic message (symbolized by the scroll) will be sweet, and yet also sorrowful. It will contain comfort, and yet it will also be very unsettling.

10:11 Again, John is told to prophesy about many peoples, nations, languages, and rulers.

Chapter 11

This chapter begins with a mention of God's temple in verse 1. It is worth noting that for John, as for many other early Christians, the word temple did not refer to a specific place (for example, the temple in Jerusalem) but had come to symbolize the presence of God's people. We witness this usage today in that Jews frequently refer to their local synagogues as "temples" because they are a place where they can encounter the presence of God, which was the purpose of the original temple. John stretches the metaphor a little to represent the wider Christian community, for he sees the community as the place where God resides.

> ■ The act of measuring God's temple is really the act of taking stock of the Christian community. Do they measure up? By extension, we might ask ourselves the same question. Do we measure up? What kinds of things might one look for as signs that we measure up?

11:2 There is great confusion about the reference to "42 months." The number is given in an archaic Hebrew form: "a time [a year] and times [2 years] and half a time [6 months]." Such specific numbers suggest that something specific is meant by them, but what? The simple and most honest answer is that we don't know, and thus any answer is a guess. But here are some possibilities:

■ Sticking with numerology, this three-and-a-half-year period could be half of perfection (represented by the number seven). Thus, half of a perfect or complete amount of time.

■ It could be intended more as a multiplication of six times seven, suggesting perfection (seven) not quite succeeding – being multiplied by six instead of by a more perfect number.

■ The number 42 also equals three times 14, which is given as the number of cycles in the genealogy of Matthew 1:1–17 (14 generations from Abraham to David, 14 from David to the Babylonian exile, and 14 from the exile to Jesus). While many scholars question the historicity of this – the numbers don't really work – the symbolism of it may well of have been intended. Does John mean 42 months (shorter periods of time) to be like the 42 generations of "waiting" for the Christ? Does he mean that we will wait for him again for a similar – but much shorter – amount of time?

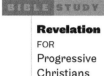
■ The number 42 is the Hebrew numerology for David, the great king whom Jesus was seen to represent.

■ Coincidentally (or not), this was the length of time that Antiochus Epiphanes ruled Israel with an iron fist, desecrating the temple and oppressing the people. He had a massive ego and seemed to defy everything that was godly. These things occurred in the mid-160s BCE, and thus were relatively recent in history. John may be seeing clear parallels to the events of his own time.

11:3 "**two witnesses...for one thousand two hundred sixty days**" The number here is another way of saying 42 months (three and a half years). Two witnesses were needed to testify in court. Presumably, these two witnesses are pointing out how Jerusalem has failed to live up to God's hopes; the reference in verse 8 to "where their Lord was crucified" seems to make it clear that this is Jerusalem.

> To me, it is clear that the real sin of Sodom is radical inhospitality, or turning one's back upon the strangers and the neediest in our midst. Rather than welcoming travelling sojourners into their homes and feeding them, the men of Sodom wanted to gang rape them and exert their power over them.
> – Rev. Patrick S. Cheng, PhD

11:8 "**spiritually called Sodom and Egypt**" These two places epitomized two horrific patterns of evil in the history of Israel. Sodom is commonly believed to have been condemned for homosexuality, but later references in scripture indicate it was destroyed for not providing hospitality, which was generally seen as the most important commandment in the Hebrew tradition. Egypt, of course, was recognized as the place where the Hebrew people had been enslaved and had suffered horrid abuse by slave masters. Together these two references symbolize the worst of all places, and they are used symbolically here to refer to the city of Jerusalem – a place that should have been the dwelling place of God, but that has been ruined by its "cheating" on God.

11:9–13 Three and a half days repeats the pattern established with the prior reference to three and a half years.

If this reference is to a time of persecution and devastation (which would make sense), then it is intriguing that the time period keeps getting shorter. In other words, the worst will be over soon. Verse 14 bears this out.

11:15–19 A great, triumphal scene is presented. This is a good news passage, a feel good passage. The worst appears to be over. Christ will rule forever and ever. The tone is so positive that it feels like we have reached the end of the book. The final verse seems to indicate that all the bad is over. Of course it's not – either in terms of the book of Revelation as a whole (there will be 11 more chapters, most of which contain bad news) and in terms of real life (so often when we think everything will be good, something bad happens). Perhaps John is suggesting that life will always be like this – some good, some bad. The good news is that God is with us through everything.

11:16 Remember the 24 elders from the first scene in the heavenly throne room? Here they are again, worshipping God.

Closing Thoughts

One theme in these chapters is that the earth is punishing us. In this era of climate change, when some parts of the planet are undergoing huge shifts, to what extent do you share this perception? How have we been responding to climate change as a society? How might we respond?

Revelation 12 – 14

In this session we notice that the style of Revelation shifts rather dramatically. Rather than plagues and trumpets, we now encounter a narrative scene that involves two women, a dragon, and a beast from the sea. All of this, we shall discover, is a cleverly veiled story about what it is like to live under the heavy foot of Rome. But God will triumph, as John reminds us continually.

Chapter 12

There is a well-known story from the island of Delos, near Patmos where John was imprisoned. In that story, a dragon called Python tried to kill the primeval king Apollo at birth. King Apollo's mother was named *Roma*. John recasts this story in light of the story of Christ, bringing in symbolism from one of the ancient creation stories (Genesis 2 and 3) for good measure.

12:1 The woman here clearly appears to be Mary, the mother of Jesus. Yet John also seems to want to imply that it is Israel, the "mother of humanity," or that it is the church as community, which "mothers" us as individuals to be the body of Christ.

> **Dragons are seen as symbols of destruction, and for good reason – they breathe fire, and fire destroys. Thus they are the antithesis of God, who is a creator.**
> ■ **What forces of destruction exist in our world? Do you think they are the antithesis of God?**

Mary

Mary, the mother of Jesus, is frequently portrayed on a crescent moon, often with a crown of 12 stars around her head. Although this is often overlooked, frequently a serpent or dragon is depicted under the moon. The image comes from Revelation 12:1.

Another powerful version of this image, "Our Lady of Guadalupe," can be found in the Basilica of Guadalupe in Mexico City. The image in the basilica stems from a series of alleged appearances Mary made in that area in 1531.

While "Our Lady of Quadalupe" has its foundation in Revelation 12:1, it was believed to be a powerful way to counter many aspects of Aztec culture. That Mary would reflect the sun seemed to challenge the power of the Aztec sun god. Her bent knee suggests she is praying not only with her hands but with her whole body, which paralleled Aztec custom. The jasmine flower on her tunic appears over her womb; this symbol of the great god Ometéotl suggested that even the Aztec god chose not to remain distant, but to be symbolically born on earth. The origins of the name "Mexico" in Aztec mean "centre of the moon," which is where Mary stands. Lastly, in place of the serpent or dragon we see an angel with eagle's wings. The Aztecs believed that the eagle delivered the blood of the sacrificed to the gods; this image suggests that Mary – and the one in her womb, who would shed blood for the world – renders the eagle's role obsolete.

Revelation
FOR
Progressive
Christians

This image of Our Lady
of Guadalupe, though
inspired by Revelation
12:1, depicts Mary in
the context of early
Aztec spirituality, and
was seen by many as a
divine lesson in this
regard.

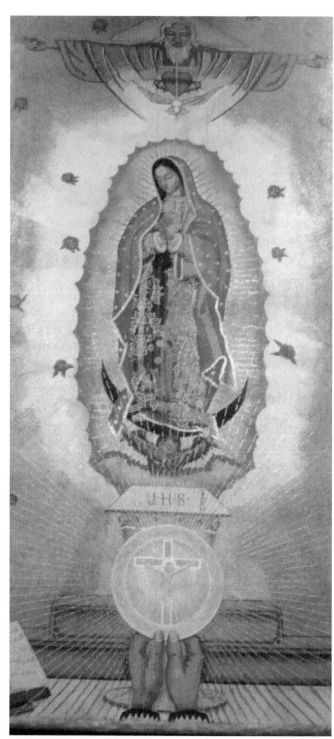

12:4–6 The woman is in the act of giving birth, clearly to the Christ. The dragon (representing evil) is eager to devour the child, but God intervenes. The woman flees to the desert for 1,260 days (three and a half years), a short period of suffering. It may help to remember that the desert was not seen as a negative place in the scriptures – perhaps because it encompassed so much of the land.

12:7–9 Enter the archangel Michael, who fights the dragon – also known as the devil or the accuser – who is not cast into eternal evil, but simply neutralized. This image is powerful: evil need not be banished forever; we simply need to know how to put it in its place.

Many people have spoken of "Satan" as if it were a proper name, but in the Bible it is not. We have John Milton to thank for elevating the word "satan" to the status of a being, in his work *Paradise Lost*. In scripture, "satan" is simply a word for "accuser." It refers to one who is not so much the epitome of evil as one who is diametrically opposed to God. One of the clearest examples of this is in the narrative portion of the book of Job (chapter 1), where God and the "accuser" are chatting. They are not enemies, as such, but the accuser perpetually challenges God. Whenever we seek to challenge God in this way, to doubt God or to take a position on the opposite side of God, we are playing the role of a "satan." In other words, in the Bible, satan is never a little red creature with a tail and a pitchfork. That particular character is simply the stuff of artists and cartoons.

■ **How do you understand the role of evil in the Bible?**
■ **Is evil a force that is a constant threat?**
■ **How would you depict evil?**

12:13–17 The dragon is not happy about being banished to the earth, and so it goes off in search of the woman. But she escapes, for "a time, and times, and half a time" (three and a half years). This time reference harkens back to the reference to 42 months in Revelation 11:2. There we saw it as a possible symbolic reference to the genealogy of Jesus and his birth, where 42 represents the number of generations between Adam and Jesus. (See page 57.) When the dragon gets too frustrated, it goes off to make war on the rest of the woman's children – perhaps an image of the evil that challenges the church from the outside.

> ■ Chapter 12 is, for all intents and purposes, a fairy tale that carries a lot of powerful meaning. Does calling it a fairy tale – and seeing it in that light – diminish or enlarge it for you?
> ■ What other "once upon a time" stories can you think of that carry deep meaning?

Chapter 13

12:18 – 13:1 This is one sentence and describes a beast coming up, out of the sea. This is a thinly veiled image of Rome. There were ten Roman provinces and, in theory, there were seven "great" emperors or Caesars. The blasphemous names refer to the fact that Caesar referred to himself as "Divine," "Son of God," and "Lord." For Christians, these titles were blasphemous because they belonged only to Jesus, not to any earthly ruler.

13:2–4 The beasts listed here come from the book of Daniel. Many Jews saw Rome as Daniel's fourth beast.

Who were the seven emperors?

We simply cannot know with any certainty which Romans emperors are being referred to in Revelation – with the exception that we are 99% certain that the number 666 refers to Caesar Nero. (See "Numbers and Numerology" on p. 91.)

There were more than seven emperors no matter how one counts them. However, if one eliminates the four who ruled for less than a year each, then Domitian (during whose reign Revelation was being written) would have been the seventh.

Some scholars suggest that the "eighth emperor" refers to Nero Redivivus, the name given to "Nero come-back-from-the-dead," as told about in a popular legend of the time. Sort of like those who imagine Hitler living on in Argentina, some people thought that Nero did not die in Rome, but lived on in the East and would come back someday with an army across the Euphrates. For many, Nero Redivivus summed up all that was bad and evil about Rome in general.

13:5–6 The beast referred to here is undoubtedly the Emperor Nero, who was considered the absolute pinnacle of anti-Christian evil. Nero had no problem killing people – he even executed his own mother – and is thought to have arranged for Rome to be burned to pave the way for his great construction projects. Moreover, he enjoyed the sport of persecuting Christians. This began in earnest in the year 64 CE, and continued until Nero was killed in 68 CE. For this reason alone, Christians despised him and assumed he was the essence of all that was wrong with the world.

**If you have been told that God is some kind of punishing, capricious, angry bastard with a killer surveillance system who is basically always disappointed with you for being a human being, then you have been lied to. The church has failed you.
– Rev. Nadia Bolz-Weber**

The one who spoke with authority for 42 months was probably Antiochus Epiphanes, who had persecuted the Jews in a similar way some 250 years earlier.

13:7 "It was also allowed" Notice how things only seem to happen when God allows them.

13:8–9 Again, we are reminded that some will suffer, and some will be killed – and life will go on.

People are often surprised to learn that the word "Antichrist" – so often associated with the number 666 and book of Revelation – does not appear anywhere in the text.

666

While often thought to refer to the "Antichrist" or "the beast," it is worth noting that Revelation says the number 666 refers to a person. This is hardly surprising; in the ancient world, people used a system known as *gematria* wherein numbers were used for letters, words, or phrases. This yields Nero in two ways:

■ The most common number presented in the ancient Greek manuscripts is 666, which, using *gematria*, becomes "Nero Caesar" in Hebrew.

■ A small number of manuscripts have adjusted this and instead of 666 they present 616, which is "Nero Caesar" in Greek.

■ Yet an even smaller series of manuscripts – generally discredited because the vast majority give one of the other numbers – lists this number as 606, which using the same system as above equals Caligula. Caligula was another Roman emperor who was noted not only for persecuting Christians, but for persecuting whomever he disliked. Known for horrendous mood swings, he would lash out and kill vast numbers of people. He was clearly unpopular, however, most scholars agree that the number 666 refers to Nero.

13:11–14 This passage refers to a number of events that happened, or were thought to have happened. Some people in Rome appeared to be sympathetic to the Christian cause (looked like a lamb), but then they spoke or acted like a dragon. A great fire came down from heaven: the "divine" fire that burned but did not destroy Rome. And a beast was wounded, but came to life again. This refers to Emperor Nero, who was believed to have died – records clearly indicate he was murdered in 68 CE – but whom many believed would come back to life.

There is something quite intriguing about this number when one applies Hebrew numerology: seven is perfection, and three is balance or completion. By default, six is imperfection, the antithesis of perfection. Thus three sixes in a row seems to represent perfect imperfection; ironically, Nero fits the bill perfectly.

It should be noted that the number 666 appears in many other religious contexts. In the Baha'i faith, the number 666 refers to the year that Muawiyah I became Caliph, or leader, in 661 CE, which by most scholarly calculations would have been 666 years after the birth of Jesus (generally calculated as happening in 4 or 5 BCE. Kabbalistic Judaism believes that 666 represents the creation and perfection of the world. The world was created in six days; there are six cardinal directions (north, south, east, west, up, down); six is also the numerical value of one of the letters of God's name. Jehovah's Witnesses believe that the beast identified by the number 666 is the world's unified governments opposed to God.

What interpretations of 666 have you encountered?

13:17 This refers to the fact that only Roman citizens – which most Jews and most Christians were not – could do business. This was a huge frustration to Jews and Christians who were thus treated as lower-class. Jews had the "sign" of circumcision, and Christians the invisible sign of baptism, but this was little comfort to those who saw numerous economic possibilities slip through their hands because they did not have a certificate of Roman citizenship. And they blamed Emperor Nero, who was only too happy with the situation.

13:18 The number 666 has been stigmatized and avoided throughout history; there are hotels that will not have this room number, and many jurisdictions will not issue licence plates with this number. People are often surprised to learn that the word "Antichrist" – so often associated with the number 666 – does not appear anywhere in the text. So to whom does it refer? A clue is the line, "Let the one who understands calculate the beast's number for it's a human being's number." In other words, John was essentially saying, "Look, I'd risk losing my head if I named the bad guy here, but you all know who he is – anyone with half a brain can figure it out. His name is _____." And in the blank, it was as if he took the name of a popular figure and simply changed a few letters – speaking of Ronald Grump or Dustin Pluto (U.S. President Donald Trump or Canadian Prime Minister Justin Trudeau). It's a classic trick of political writing – you don't use the real name, and if anyone says "boy that sure sounds like so-and-so" you can shrug your shoulders and say, "pure coincidence." Every Christian reading this book in ancient times immediately knew this meant Nero.

Chapter 14
Chapter 14 contains some extremely difficult passages that are hard to discern. They are complicated by imag-

ery that is quite alien to us, as well as by ambiguities in name, and by extreme rhetorical hyperbole (a pool of blood as high as a horse's bridle and stretching for 200 miles, for example).

14:1 Just as chapter 13 ends with a significant number (666), chapter 14 begins with a significant number: 144,000. This number was thought by early Seventh-day Adventists to be the number of those who would be saved, and they strongly believed that something wonderful (including the end of the world) would occur when exactly 144,000 people became Adventists. A problem occurred, obviously, when their evangelistic efforts yielded a greater number. Rather than stop, they simply reinterpreted it to mean that the 144,000 were special, or that it was just a symbolic number. This last is a bit closer to reality; the number 144,000 is similar to an expression of infinity.

The meaning the Hebrews attached to numbers was more vague than the meaning we attach to numbers today. Thus, a number in the thousands could really mean infinity, or like a child might say, in the "gazillions." In other words, the number is essentially 144 (12 tribes x 12 disciples x an infinite number that includes everyone: all those who are descended from the 12 tribes of Israel, as well as all those who follow Jesus.

14:3 "a new song" Singing a new song is a common theme of hope in many of the psalms.

14:4 "weren't defiled with women" This phrase has caused no end of problems over the years! Scholars vary greatly in their understanding of this line. Some have suggested that it is in fact a scribal insertion added by someone who was copying the text, as a way of elevating celibacy. Others suggest that it refers to "spiritual purity or fidelity, meaning that it refers to those who have not

BIBLE STUDY

Revelation
FOR
Progressive
Christians

No culture can live if it attempts to be exclusive.
– Mahatma Gandhi

Peace requires everyone to be in the circle – wholeness, inclusion.
– Isabel Allende

"cheated" on God – thereby "defiling" themselves – but who have remained loyal. This is a weak interpretation, but still has some merit. Others believe the line has to do with a sense of not worrying about the need to have sex for procreation because the world was going to end soon, and so it did not matter. This interpretation could have some merit, except that the remainder of Revelation is less concerned with the end of the world and far more concerned with how we live in the meantime.

Paul, who certainly believed early in his Christian career in the pending return of Christ, promoted celibacy and in 1 Corinthians 7:9 suggested that the only reason to get married was if you were so consumed with sexual passion that you couldn't resist! Yet earlier in the very same chapter he said that married couples should have sexual relations. So the point becomes a bit more muddied.

Yet another suggestion has to do with holy war, which is at times a sub-theme running behind the stories of Revelation. When conquering a people, it was assumed that Israelite men had the right to rape conquered women. This verse could suggest that this refers to those who did not do that; the defilement here would be rape. If this is the case, this is an extremely positive and powerful statement about higher standards that is less concerned with sex and more concerned with human dignity and respect for human rights.

14:6 Here is another universal passage: proclaim good news (the gospel) to every nation, tribe, language, and people.

14:6 Babylon As noted before, this is a thinly veiled reference to Rome.

14:9–11 There is clearly some rhetoric at play in this passage, and yet the feelings are very real. For those who

Predicting the future

Bob Dylan wrote and first performed his
song "A Hard Rain's a-Gonna Fall" in Sep-
tember 1962. The date is significant because
it was later claimed that the song was
written in response to the Cuban missile
crisis, when in fact the crisis did not occur
until a month after the song was first performed. Yet the words of the song are
strangely prescient.

What do you think of writings – such as
Dylan's song, or the book of Revelation –
that seem to "predict" future events? Do you
think they are really doing that, or simply
that they are reflecting a world in which
such events could happen, or...?

conspire with Rome, and who are thus complicit in the
efforts that ultimately persecute Christians, there is no
relief. They will suffer – and so they should, the author
seems to believe. Think for a moment of those who commit treason in times of war, and how they are treated.

14:14 "Human One" Some translations render this "Son
of Man," which immediately can make us think it refers
to Jesus, but that is not always the case in the Bible. "Human One" is used often in the Bible, particularly in Daniel,
simply as a way to say "human being." In other words,
John may be using "Human One" to refer to Jesus, or
simply to clarify that he's not talking about an "angelic
being" or a "mythical beast."

14:14–20 The first harvest (verse 16) seems to be of faithful souls, although this is a conjecture that some scholars
dispute. Clearly the second harvest is of unfaithful souls,

who are trampled in the winepress of God's anger. This action occurs outside the city, which would be the place where Gentiles would be judged. Yet it is also the place where Jesus was crucified. Is there a link? We simply don't know.

14:20 "Two hundred miles" or 1600 stadia The number 1600 is a square number, which might imply perfection, or completeness, suggesting that this is a complete pouring out of blood. In other words, no other sacrifice would be necessary.

15:1 After encountering God's anger in this way, it helps to read the reassurance in 15:1 that God's anger comes to an end.

Closing Thoughts

The passionate anger of God displayed in chapter 14 presents an image we may not like. But a parallel example can help. Imagine a parent who is angry with something their child has done. (If you've ever been around a two-year-old or a teenager, you may know a bit of what this can be like.) The parent is so furious they lash out: "So help me, if you do that again I'll slap you within an inch of your life."

In that instant, in that one single moment, they may well mean it. Yet 99.9% of the time they do not. Such is the nature of God's anger, as frequently presented to us in Revelation, and in other scripture such as in Hosea 11:5–9, which we looked in Session 1. (See "The Wrath of God," page 22.)

■ How do you understand the many passages like this in Revelation, which speak of God's anger?

Revelation 15 – 18

In this session we encounter the final set of plagues, which are somewhat contained and which have an eerie familiarity to them. We also read a rather entertaining image of Rome as a prostitute, and a brief editorial on some of the consequences of Rome's demise.

Chapter 15

15:1 We begin where we left off, with the awareness that God's anger will come to an end.

15:2–3 This first image depicts those who have survived the suffering of the previous plagues and who are now singing the song of Moses (the great leader and lawgiver of the people who experienced his own set of hardships), and of the Lamb.

> ■ Note that the reason given for worshipping the Lamb, or Christ, relates to his acts of justice. When you hear talk of all nations worshipping Christ, how often is justice the focal point?

15:3b–4 The "**song of the Lamb**" is a great hymn of praise that recognizes that Christ is just and true. The song looks forward to the day when all nations will come and worship the Christ, for his acts of justice will be revealed.

15:5–8 The final plagues consist of God's anger carried by seven angels in seven bowls. The use of the number

seven for both the angels and the bowls may imply completion, the end of the plagues, although we have seen this number used before with the other plagues. However, the significance of the bowls may be that they are finite, or that what they contain is finite; a bowl can only hold so much, after all. This could suggest that the amount of God's anger that remains is limited, and in the grand scheme of things quite small. However, given that everything in the sea dies, and the evil Parthians from the east invade across the Euphrates, amongst other things, the "smallness" of these plagues seems not so small.

Chapter 16

There is a great deal of discussion of blood at the beginning of chapter 16. It helps to remember that blood while viewed here as destructive, because it poisons the sea and the rivers, is also viewed as positive in other places. Touching the blood of another could render one ritually unclean, and yet blood was understood to be the source of life in ancient Hebrew culture. Whereas we often speak of the "breath of life," they would speak of the "blood of life." Many images used in the Bible have that same, dual nature. For example, we need salt to survive, yet too much will kill us; we use fire for cooking, light, and heat, and yet we all know its power to destroy.

16:9 The people do not change their hearts and lives, much like the Egyptian pharaoh at the time of the Exodus, whose heart was repeatedly hardened despite the devastating power of the plagues inflicted upon him and his people.

16:12 This probably happened once, and the people were terrified it would happen again. When Cyrus was invading Babylon, the river Euphrates had been diverted into a canal, and thus he was able to get across. The significance of the Euphrates in Revelation is that it was the eastern boundary of the Roman Empire. Beyond the Euphrates lived the Parthians, and early Christians (or at least John) believed that the Parthians were to be feared. Thus, the notion of the Euphrates drying up can be seen as an expression of paranoia.

> ■ Jesus is presented in a variety of ways throughout the book of Revelation: as lamb, as ruler, and, in chapter 16, as judge. How does your understanding of Jesus shift when you apply each of these names to him?
> ■ What are other ways in which you understand Jesus?

16:16 "Harmagedon" Of all the names in the book of Revelation, this one (often spelled Armageddon) has probably taken on more baggage than any of the others. In fact, so much mythology has grown up around the idea or concept of Armageddon as an *event* that many people may not be aware that it refers to an actual *place*. In Hebrew, *Harmagedon* refers to Tel (or Mount) Megiddo, or to the city of Megiddo.

It was located to the southwest of the Sea of Galilee, near Mount Carmel. This last fact is intriguing, because Mount Carmel is where Elijah defeated the prophets of Baal, after taunting them – a story intended to show that the God of the Jews is much stronger than all other gods, who aren't really gods at all. Thus, the mention of Harmagedon here could be to remind the people that someday, they will be able to defeat the powers of Rome the same way that Elijah defeated the prophets of Baal. The mention of the city might also be simply to jog people's memories. Other battles had taken place there over the years, thus, saying "there will be a battle at Megiddo" may be like saying, "Let's send the president to Dallas." The latter would immediately conjure up the memory of what happened to President Kennedy in Dallas. In other words, it would be like saying "the same thing is going to happen again." Significantly, Harmagedon is mentioned in Revelation as a passing comment, without a lot of fuss.

16:17–21 This is another highly rhetorical passage – the conjuring of 100-pound hailstones and the mention of islands running away in fear are clearly not meant to be taken literally but are figures of speech. The seventh angel pours out his bowl, and pronounces, "It is done." A multitude of horrible things happen, and then it is over.

Chapter 17

17:1–2 Once again, the "great whore" is Rome. To say that the kings of the earth have slept with her is to say that they have courted her; they have fostered relationships with her and they are drunk with the wine of her whoring. In other words, they are overcome by the apparent success they experience from associating with and accommodating Rome.

17:3–6 The scarlet beast upon which the woman (Rome) sits is the *history* of Rome, a history that is bloody and that includes ten provinces that were dominated by seven "great" emperors. The woman wears purple (a sign of wealth) and scarlet (a sign of sexual immorality) and shines with the glitter of gold and pearls. But, to use the street vernacular – which is essentially what Revelation does – she is nothing but a "two-bit whore." She has abused the saints of the church, which is a mild euphemism for having persecuted them.

Remembering John's audience

Sometimes when we do not know the answer to a question, we guess, which is okay except when we later try to turn our guesses into "facts." It helps to remember *why* John was writing. To quote biblical scholar Eugene Boring from his book *Revelation: A Bible Commentary for Teaching and Preaching*, "John is writing a pastoral letter to address the immediate problem of his reader-hearers, not a puzzle for later readers." In other words, John isn't writing for, or thinking about, those of us who are trying to understand this 2,000 years later and from halfway around the world. He was writing to assure people of his own time. Thus, things like the identity of the emperor were not an issue for him because the people he was writing for knew who the emperor was. The fact that we can't always figure these things out is *our* problem, not John's. Beyond that, to try to identify the emperors is to miss the larger point; the emperors were bad and were enemies of Christianity.

Without assuming that Revelation was written to address our modern world, who today might be the equivalent of a Roman emperor?

17:8 "was and is not and will again be present" This line is vague at best, but may refer to the previously mentioned Nero Redivivus, or Nero who-is-coming-back-to-life. Some people thought he had not yet returned, while others believed that he had been reincarnated in Emperor Domitian, who was probably emperor when this book was written.

Though the phrase is vague in that we can't know exactly which emperor is being referred to, it *is* clear that John is referring to an emperor of Rome, and none of them were friends of the Christian community. Thus, by extension, neither were they friends of God and Christ. This seems to be confirmed in verse 14, where John writes, "They will make war on the Lamb, but the Lamb will emerge victorious, for he is Lord of lords and King of kings." In other words, Rome is nothing compared to God.

A minority of scholars believe that the reference to Babylon in chapter 17 does *not* represent Rome, but rather Jerusalem. This conclusion is not well-supported. However, those who like this theory base it on the fact that Jerusalem should have been the epitome of all things godly, but instead had cheapened itself by giving in to evil – in other words, sleeping around. Instead of standing up for God's justice and righteousness, Jerusalem has given in to the popular gods and notions of the day, and this is doubly wrong.

Chapter 18

This chapter opens with the scene of the great whore falling to ruin. Merchants and rulers of the earth have consorted with her, to their peril.

18:2 "**She has become a home for demons**" For the early readers of this text, the meaning of this reference would have been abundantly clear because it was believed that demons lived among ruins. Thus, this is simply a way of saying she has become nothing more than a heap of rubble – a great insult to place upon the once-mighty Rome.

18:4–8 This is quite amazing poetry in the original Greek text, with a lot of alliteration.

18:6 There should be no limit to the punishment Rome gets, for all she has done wrong. The pain that the church has suffered leads to this call for great revenge.

18:8–10 Rome thinks she is invincible and so will be especially shocked when she is brought down. Similarly, the rulers who consorted with her will be horrified when they realize she has no future.

18:11–14 The long list of items here is intriguing, if for no reason other than that they are all imports and thus are things that only the wealthiest people (thus primarily non-Christians) could ever dream of affording. This passage bespeaks the anger of the dispossessed. For those of us in the developed world, it can be difficult to visit places in the developing world where items we take for granted are beyond the economic hopes and dreams of the vast majority of people.

> ■ Imagine for a moment that you have lost your wealth, and are forced to live in the kind of poverty experienced by people in Sudan or El Salvador or Venezuela, for example. What might that feel like?

18:17 "in just one hour" Instantly.

18:19 "they threw dust on their heads" This is a traditional sign of repentance or sorrow. Essentially, the people who had once had dealings with Rome are now separating themselves from it and saying, "Gee, God, we aren't like her. Don't judge us the same way." Like slimy politicians, in an instant they seem to have shifted their allegiance from consorting with Rome to condemning it.

Another way to read this, however, is that they were mourning Rome's demise, or rather, the demise of their profits.

18:21–24 This passage describes, with great flourish and poetic detail, the destruction of Rome, presumably in the near future. The early readers of this book would have found great comfort in this passage. It's an ultimate "good riddance," for it suggests that Rome will be gone for good.

Closing Thoughts

As modern Christians, we may struggle with the pronouncement that Rome should be punished, or we may not. Because we are reading this text as part of our own spiritual heritage, and because it is about events that happened long ago and far away, we may separate ourselves from the feelings Revelation portrays so dramatically.

At the same time, we may be aware of the destructive potential of harbouring sentiments like those described in 18:6. The desire for revenge, for example, places us on a slippery slope. Many people today also long for revenge, and we've seen the devastation such misguided anger can cause.

What is the difference between Christians in ancient times calling for revenge on Rome, and groups today who call for revenge on the West because of the persecution they perceive we have enacted upon them?

Revelation 19 – 22

In the final few chapters, Revelation moves toward a triumphant vision of what will happen following the collapse of Rome and the church's other enemies. These final chapters focus on the aftermath, and celebrating the great New Jerusalem that will replace the tired, filthy, corrupt Rome.

Chapter 19

19:1–3 There is great rejoicing, because in the end God triumphs and earthly wealth and power fail.

> ■ **What is it like to reflect on this image of wealth and power failing given that, compared to much of the world, we are the wealthy and powerful ones?**

19:3 "**smoke goes up from her forever and always**" This refers to perpetual smoke rising from the destroyed body of Rome. It is also one of the sources of our "modern" notion of hell as a place of eternal fire. The ultimate punishment in the Judaism of this time was to throw the dead body of someone who was guilty of a grave sin or transgression onto the fires in the garbage dump because not only was it a grave insult, it meant that the person would no longer have a body and thus the Messiah could not resurrect them.

19:7 When the end comes, Jesus will marry the Christian church. This lifts up a common image of ancient Israel, that God and the nation would be married. The Hebrew word is

beulah, which led to numerous hymns celebrating "Beulah land" as the place where the people were married, or re-married, to God. This was juxtaposed with images of sleeping around with other gods, or with other temptations, which would cause God to want to divorce the people.

19:11 — 21:1 This is the first of several uses of the phrase, "Then I saw..." to introduce a vision. The repetition suggests continuity and a regulated flow of visions and ideas. This may have been added to help smooth out a text that, towards the end, becomes rather jumbled.

19:13 Some scholars think the blood referred to here was the blood of Parthians; this is a way of saying that Jesus has destroyed the worst of the worst.

The proclamation "hallelujah!" is a loud word of praise to God. What makes you want to shout "hallelujah"?

19:17–18 It was common practice, in times of war, to eat a feast among the dead and dying of your enemies. As the dying cried out for mercy and assistance, the victors would munch on a great meal. This was a way of emphasizing that the spoils of war had indeed gone to the victors. Today, it seems strange, even repulsive, to imagine Christ doing this, to imagine Christ inviting *anyone* to such a macabre event. Of course, nothing in Revelation is to be understood literally. The language and imagery are symbolic, and mean "they got no less than they deserved."

19:20 "lake that burns with sulfur" While some people get very excited by this image, the most likely meaning is simply "a lake that stinks."

Chapter 20

Chapters 20 — 22 are quite jumbled; they could probably have used a good editor! Some pieces get repeated and some seem genuinely out of place. In this study, we follow the traditional biblical order.

The Anchor Bible is a series of commentaries that was published by Doubleday Press beginning in the 1970s. Their volume on Revelation, by Josephine Massyngberde Ford, was considered quite controversial for much of its take on the book. However, Ford provides an intriguing option for ordering the last three chapters of the book, as follows:

20:1–3
21:9–27, 8, 22:1–2
22:14–15
20:4–15
21:1–4c
22:3–5
21:5a, 4d, 5b, 6, 7
22:6–7a, 8–13, 7b, 17b, 18–19

She then follows this with the first three chapters of the book, and concludes with 22:16–17a, 20–21.

While not generally accepted as correct, still there is some merit to this approach, and some argue that the text flows much more logically when read in this order.

20:1 "a huge chain" This term could also mean leg irons.

20:2–3 The expression "threw...locked...sealed" is akin to our modern expression "signed, sealed, and delivered." The accuser, who was formerly a danger to the Jews (because he challenged the Jewish God) is now being kept away from the Gentiles (the nations) because they are now included in God's community.

20:4–6 Some are resurrected sooner. These are the ones who are deserving because they have given their lives for the cause of the faith.

20:7 The idea of a thousand years probably just means "a long time" or infinity, which would imply that it won't ever come back. When the thousand years are over, "Satan" will be released from his prison. Or, in other words, bad will come again someday. But not for a long, long

The end of the millennium

Not too long ago, many people got excited about the year 2,000. Great predictions of doomsday were made and many people got caught up in a sense of panic, which was both intriguing and silly. It's perhaps especially intriguing with respect to those whose fears were based on what's written in Revelation. After all, the end of millennium did not come 1,000 years after Revelation was written, but 2,000 years after the fact (though if Revelation was written in 95 CE, then it was really only 1,905 years).

More to the point, although from a scientific perspective a "year" represents one complete orbit of the Earth around the sun, how we count them – and how we've broken them into epochs or periods, BCE and CE for example – is arbitrary. There have also been those who have "fiddled" with time. Pope Gregory XIII chopped 10 days out of the year in 1582, when he instituted the switch from the Julian calendar to the Gregorian calendar, which is the most widely used calendar today. Not all countries made the switch at the same time, however, and the later the switch occurred, the more days had to be omitted during the year of the change. Turkey, which was the most recent country to make the switch (on January 1, 1927), had to drop 13 days in that year.

time. When strife does return, we are told in 20:8–10 that it won't last. It may be worth noting that John used chapters 6 – 18 to speak of three and a half years, and now speaks of 1,000 years in only three verses.

20:11–14 At the end of this series of visions comes the most climactic one of all: Death is destroyed! The dead are judged on the basis of how they lived their lives. Unfortunately, for those whose names don't appear in the book of life, the second death, the "lake of fire," awaits.

■ Which do you think is harder: to judge someone or to forgive them?
■ Even here at the end of Revelation, we encounter God's judgement. Or to say it another way, the writer of Revelation clearly does not embrace a universal understanding of "salvation." Some are "saved" and some are not. Although this is a common understanding among conservative Christians today, do you sense a shift towards a more universal understanding of "salvation" in theology and the church?
■ Does this understanding appeal to you? Why?
■ Why might some people find it more difficult to give up the idea of judgement (God's or their own) in favour of forgiveness and/or an idea of salvation that includes everyone?

Chapters 21 and 22

Many people are familiar with portions of chapters 21 and 22 of Revelation as these texts are often read at Christian funerals. Selections from these chapters are also occasionally read in Sunday worship. In some ways, these

chapters return us to the beginning in that certain images are repeated, and yet we have moved beyond the earlier judgement and death, and now face John's vision of a life-filled future.

21:1 In the good news of the final vision, the sea is gone. For a variety of reasons, the Jews were afraid of the ocean.

21:3 "God's dwelling is here with humankind" This is a key thought. Instead of needing a temple in which to reside, God has chosen to dwell in our midst. This image also appears at the beginning of the gospel of John, in the writer's statement that the "Word became flesh and made his home among us" (1:14).

21:4 "Death will be no more" Clearly this is an eschatological statement about a future time beyond current existence, not a statement about the lived reality of readers then or now.

21:6a The reference to God being the Alpha and the Omega – the beginning and the end – echoes chapter 1.

21:6b If we have needs, God will supply them.

21:7-8 This is a rather horrid image of the second death that awaits those who engage in a variety of behaviours. It is worth noting that the list of negative things – from being cowardly to lying – seems to parallel the activities of those who consorted with Rome.

21:9 The bride of the Lamb – the church – is presented as an obvious contrast to Rome, the great whore.

21:20–21 The description of the holy city defies the imagination. It is magnificent – a huge and perfect square – 1,500 miles on each side.

To put that in some perspective, it is roughly the distance between Jerusalem and Rome. Would John have known that? Possibly. If so, this might be another way John shows that God's realm completely subsumes or encompasses all that came before it. Alternatively, it may simply be an exaggeration, a way of saying "this city is bigger than you can ever imagine." Not a bad image for the city of God, either way!

The 12 stones listed as forming the foundation of the city approximate or emulate those associated with the ancient tribes of Israel; thus, the 12 tribes have been "reborn" in an amazing new way.

Lastly, we are told that the main street is made of pure gold transparent as glass. This of course makes no sense taken literally; the point is simply that the new Jerusalem is lavish beyond anyone's wildest dreams.

21:22 Harking back to verse 3 where it was implied, here John states clearly that there is no temple, because God dwells here. God is no longer distant (if God ever really was) but is now as close as next door.

21:24 **"The nations will walk by its light"** Other apocalyptic writings speak of a war between Jews and Gentiles, but this vision includes all.

21:25 The gates will never be shut by day, and there will be no night – in other words, the gates will always stay open; *anyone can enter at any time.*

21:27 We must be careful not to read what is not there. The statement that nothing unclean will ever enter, nor anyone who does what is vile or deceitful, does not mean that those people don't have the option to change. In other words, there is the possibility for all to change their lives.

■ What might it have meant to those who first read Revelation to be told that death was no more for them? What does it mean to you?
■ What does the image of the New Jerusalem mean to you?
■ Is this something for which you long?
■ Do you believe the New Jerusalem is something we can dream of, or hope for, or are we called to build it ourselves?

Chapter 22

Flowing through the middle of the city will be a river of life-giving water. For a people who lived in a desert area, and who frequently spent much of their waking hours seeking water or fetching water, this would have been astonishingly good news that is difficult for us in the modern developed world to get our heads around. We turn on a tap and water comes out, so we don't really know what it is to live without it. For John's audience, the opposite was true. So for them, the image of a river flowing through their midst would have been a natural or obvious description of what the best possible of all worlds might look like, which is no doubt why John chose the image. He knows his audience and he knows what they long for. Beyond that, the river produces fruits of all kinds, and the leaves provide healing for all peoples, images that again speak to what would have been their most natural and profound desires.

As before, John reminds his readers that God will be with them, they will see God's face – this is new! – and there will be no more night. In other words, God will be present in life-giving ways they cannot even begin to imagine.

22:7 "I'm coming soon" These words appear to come directly from Jesus' mouth, though obviously they were written as part of John's description of his dream. Even so, they have caused no end of complications over the centuries. The simple fact is that John's vision has not come true, given that he wrote Revelation sometime around the year 95 CE. Does that mean John was wrong? Or does it mean perhaps that we have misunderstood John's words or his intentions?

The statement that Jesus was coming soon was not meant to predict anything, but was undoubtedly meant to encourage those who were struggling and suffering. To these people, John was essentially saying, "Hang in there just a little longer."

■ We often seek to take the words about "Jesus coming soon" literally. But maybe they are not meant that way at all. Perhaps we are to understand that, when we live a Christ-like life, Jesus is here. In other words, if we follow Christ, Christ is present – and by extension, if we do not, he is not.
■ How do you understand the notion of Jesus coming soon?

22:8 John reminds us that he saw this vision. This is a standard way for an ancient writer to "authenticate" their text.

22:11 This is an odd little couplet that some scholars think is inserted; it does not make a lot of sense, and its language is somewhat alien to the rest of the text.

22:15 A list of people is given – people who are "outside." Does this mean they are condemned to stay out there forever, or only until they change? Often we want to read this – or are told to read this – as meaning "you'll have to stay out forever because you're bad," but the text does not say that; it may well mean "you can stay out until you change your attitude." This could be similar to a parent who disciplines a child by saying "no dessert for you until you change your attitude." This does not mean, of course, that the parent is condemning the child, but simply disciplining them – and probably hoping that this will provide a bit of incentive for them to change their minds.

22:17 Those who are thirsty (for God's life-giving water) are invited to come and receive it as a gift.

22:18–19 This was a standard way to end a text in ancient times. The reality is that Revelation would have to be copied by hand, and so there was always the risk that a copyist would seek to "improve" the text. However, it was thought that adding a threat or curse such as this would prohibit any tampering.

A Final Closing Thought

The book of Revelation has puzzled people for almost 2,000 years. Yet there seems to be some powerful material here – reminders that God is with us, and will be with us, no matter what. Reminders that God, and not the evil powers of this world, will triumph in the end. Reminders that the righteous will prevail, and God will be with us. Always. Until the end of time.

- ■ What parts of Revelation did you like?
- ■ What parts have left you wondering?
- ■ What parts do you wish were not there?
- ■ What parts would you change if you could?
- ■ What parts would you like to learn more about?

Numbers and Numerology

Jewish numerology is very "primitive" – that is to say, it is basic and does not involve much math. In the tradition known as *gematria*, or the spiritual interpretation of numbers, Judaism found certain numbers to be significant, but did not develop or write about higher mathematics until well after the Greeks, Egyptians, or Phoenicians, for example. Additionally, early Christianity was influenced not only by Jewish numerology, but also the various understandings of numbers in some of the other traditions around them.

The significance of certain numbers was understood by or carried over into early Christianity and the period in which the book of Revelation was written. Some of the spiritual significance of these basic numbers is as follows.

1 Very significant in Judaism because there is only one God. Thus it indicates unity, divinity, and wholeness.

3 Represents stability and completeness. A three-legged table not only balances, it doesn't wobble. Thus three becomes meaningful as the primary number of a "structure." Its significance carried over into Christianity, where it can be seen in the doctrine of the Trinity.

4 Four corners, four directions – this seemed to be a primary number around which many things revolved. For example, we have the list of four animals in Revelation; we have four gospels; we have four headwaters in Genesis 2 generated in Eden and spreading out to the proverbial four corners of the earth; and of course, at the time the various biblical books were written the world was thought to be flat, thus the sense of the four directions was paramount.

5 The number of protection. There are five books of Moses and five divisions in the Psalms.

6 One less than seven – another way of saying "imperfect" or "not quite there" or even "perfect failure."

7 A very powerful number in Judaism. God created the heavens and earth in seven days. The seventh day, the Sabbath, was obviously holy. Thus, seven represents "creation" but also blessing, good fortune, and even luck. Because it is such a powerful number, things tended to be grouped into sevens: there are seven patriarchs and matriarchs, the land is to lie fallow every seventh year, there are seven laws of Noah, and so on. Anything that came in groups of seven was considered holy.

8 Another number that signifies completion.

9 Three times three, thus a special number, though not often referred to.

10 Symbolizes power and good luck. There are ten commandments. It takes ten men to constitute a *minyan*, or spiritual community.

12 Represents totality, wholeness, and completion, especially of God's purpose. There are 12 tribes of Israel, and later, because of this, 12 disciples. It is four times three, both of which are significant numbers in and of themselves.

18 A very significant number in the Jewish tradition because it signifies "life," or *chai*. It is also considered the luckiest number in the Jewish tradition.

40 Can mean simply "a long time," but it is usually associated with some sort of radical transition or transformation. For example, in the story of the flood, it rained for 40 days and 40 nights; Moses spent 40 days on Mount Sinai; the Israelites spent 40 years in the desert after their escape from Egypt. In the New Testament, Jesus spent 40 days in the wilderness, where he was tempted, before beginning his ministry.

1,000 While this is a real number, for the Jews it primarily represented "a huge amount," or an infinite number. Thus, whenever we read "thousand" in the Bible, we need to be cautious. It is extremely doubtful that it ever refers to an actual "thousand."

The things that the ancient Jews believed you could do with numbers was fairly limited:

■ You could double them, which was thought to increase their "power." Thus 14 was special because it was perfection (seven) doubled.

■ You could triple them, which was extra good, because that involved the number three, which was a good number. Thus whenever there are three of something, it may well be important. In early Christianity and in Revelation in particular, because it is three renderings of six, the number 666 can be interpreted or understood to represent "perfect imperfection" or "the epitome of something that tried to be something perfect but failed miserably."

■ You could multiply by hundreds. One hundred was often used as a vague number meaning "more than you can *reasonably* count."

■ You could multiply by thousands, which was also a vague number, meaning literally "more than you can *possibly* count." This made something gargantuan. A classic example is the 144,000, which equals 12 x 12 x 1,000, or an infinite number that includes numbers of completion – a Jewish way of rendering infinity.

Babylon, Rome, and Parthia

Babylon was a major city in ancient Mesopotamia situated in the fertile plain between the Tigris and Euphrates rivers. In fact, Mesopotamia is a Greek word meaning "between the rivers." The city was built along the Euphrates and divided in equal parts along its left and right banks, with steep embankments to contain the river's seasonal floods. Babylon was originally a small Akkadian city dating from the period of the Akkadian Empire (c. 2,300 BCE).

Babylon eclipsed Nippur as the "holy city" of Mesopotamia around the time of the sixth Amorite king, Hammurabi. Babylon, the city, grew and south Mesopotamia came to be known as Babylonia. King Hammurabi was famous for formulating a legal code that was written in the day-to-day language of the people and that was displayed for any and all to read, although most people were illiterate. Such an act suggested a level of compassion that was astonishingly new, and began the concept of the rule of law, wherein people are governed by long-lasting laws, and not just by the whim of a ruler.

The Babylonian empire quickly dissolved after Hammurabi's death and Babylon spent long periods under foreign domination. After being destroyed and then rebuilt by the Assyrians, Babylon became the capital of the Neo-Babylonian Empire from 609 to 539 BCE. The Hanging Gardens of Babylon were one of the seven wonders of the ancient world. After the fall of the Neo-Babylonian Empire, the city came under the rule of the Achaemenid, Seleucid, Parthian, Roman, and Sassanid empires.

It has been estimated that Babylon was the largest city in the world from approximately 1770 to 1670 BCE, and again between approximately 612 to 320 BCE. It was perhaps the first city to reach a population above 200,000. Estimates for the maximum extent of its area range from 890 to 900 hectares (approximately 2,200 acres). The remains of the city are found in present-day Hillah, Iraq, about 85 km (50 miles) south of Baghdad, and consist of a large hill of broken mud-brick buildings and debris.

Babylon was a chic, vibrant city with a lot of flash. (Think New York City as opposed to Saskatoon.) In 605 BCE, King Nebuchadnezzar of Babylon laid siege to Jerusalem. The Jewish king refused to pay him tribute, so Nebuchadnezzar conquered Jerusalem, and took the Jews (or at least the community leaders) into exile in Babylon, where they stayed until Cyrus freed them in 539 BCE.

Some Jews returned from exile, and some wanted to stay in the big city. Over time, Babylon became in the Jewish mind the epitome of all that was evil, bad, and corrupt in society.

The significance of Babylon in the book of Revelation is that it represents Rome. Since it would have been too risky

BIBLE STUDY

Revelation
FOR
Progressive
Christians

At its greatest, the Roman Empire controlled some 6.5 million square kilometres, or 2.5 million square miles. Many signs of the empire still exist, even at its furthest reaches, as lasting testimony to its significance.

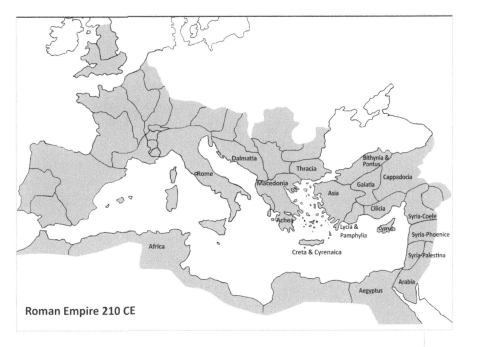

Roman Empire 210 CE

to openly criticize Rome or its government – just as it would have been risky to speak ill of the government in Nazi Germany, or of the government of the Soviet Union during the time of Stalin – people spoke about Babylon instead, and everyone understood what was meant.

The power of Rome in the time of its empire was immense. According to legend, Rome was founded by two brothers and demigods, Romulus and Remus, in about 735 BCE. Rome quickly grew to become a vibrant and powerful centre of what was then the known Western world.

As often happens, as Rome's size and grandeur grew, so did its sense of importance and the egos of its leaders. The lust for power among its leaders became enormous, and the need to solidify commonality became paramount. The famous *Pax Romana* (Roman peace) that came into being was truly noteworthy. For over 200 years – from 27 BCE to 180 CE, the entire empire knew a level of peace and prosperity that was previously unheard of. That was the good news. The bad news was that, for some, this came at a huge price as the "Roman peace" was often enforced or brought about with brutal violence.

To ensure peace and order throughout the empire, certain behaviours were required. One of these was the greeting "Caesar is lord." (Think of how Germans were required to say "Heil Hitler" as a greeting during the Third Reich.) For most people, whether or not they supported the Roman government, this was not a problem.

For Christians, however, this presented a huge problem. For them, *Jesus* was lord, so by extension Caesar was not. To say that someone other than Jesus was lord was equivalent to publicly denying their faith, and the vast majority of Christians were not prepared to do this.

The refusal of Christians to say "Caesar is lord" ruffled the feathers of Roman authorities – who could not tolerate such rebellion – and also of everyday citizens, who could not understand why this odd group would not behave like everyone else. Anti-Christian fervour grew, and thus Christians became ready scapegoats for social anger.

Historical records vary somewhat as to the level and type of discrimination experienced by Christians, largely because records kept by Christians maximized it, and records kept by Romans minimized it. We do know, however, that Rome not only tolerated but actively encouraged the mistreatment of Christians in terms of such things as employment, housing, and social norms. By some accounts, it was okay to trip a Christian, call them names, or even spit on them. We also know that some Christians were killed for sport in the arenas of the empire, often fighting lions. Whether this happened once or a thousand times is less important than simply recognizing the horror of such incidents, and the incredible fear those incidents would have conjured in other Christians.

Accordingly, Christians despised Rome and everything it epitomized. They would proudly and defiantly declare "Jesus is lord" in flagrant denial of the Roman requirement, and they often paid a steep price for such disobedience.

Parthia lay beyond the Euphrates River. Some said it didn't really start until you were east of the Tigris River. The Romans were terrified of Parthia. Their attitude towards the Parthians – fear, hatred, and paranoia – was similar to the attitude of the Jews towards the Nazis (which was completely justified), or the attitude towards Muslims in rightwing America today (not justified at all).

Expressions of hatred toward Parthia were always permitted. Beyond that, irrational fear was rampant, and stories of the horrors of Parthia grew to astounding proportions. Interestingly, this is the area that in modern times has become Iran, and attitudes to Parthia then are similar to attitudes towards Iran and other Muslim countries today.

All of which begs the question, why do we seem to so desperately need scapegoats?

Bibliography

Achtemeier, Paul J., ed. *The HarperCollins Bible Dictionary.* San Francisco: Harper San Francisco, 1996.

Arndt, William F. and Wilbur F. Gingrich. *A Greek-English Lexicon of the New Testament and other Early Christian Literature.* Chicago and London: University of Chicago Press, 1979.

Barclay, William. *Revelation: Daily Study Bible.* Toronto: GR Welch, 1976.

Boring, M. Eugene. *Revelation: Interpretation: A Bible Commentary for Teaching and Preaching.* Atlanta: John Knox Press, 1979.

Bromiley, Geoffrey W. *Theological Dictionary of the New Testament – Abridged in One Volume.* Based on the earlier work of the same title by Gerhard Kittel and Gerhard Friedrich. Trans. by Geoffrey W. Bromiley. Grand Rapids, MI: Eerdmans Publishing, 1985.

Common English Bible. Nashville: Abingdon, 2011.

Ecclesia Bible Society. *The Voice Bible: Step into the Story of Scripture.* Nashville: Thomas Nelson, 2012.

Institute for New Testament Textual Research. *The Greek New Testament,* third ed. United Bible Societies, 1975.

Levine, Amy-Jill and Marc Zvi Brettler, eds. *The Jewish Annotated New Testament: New Revised Standard Version Bible Translation.* Oxford: Oxford University Press, 2011.

Massyngberde Ford, J. *Revelation: The Anchor Bible.* Garden City, NY: Doubleday, 1975.

Peterson, Eugene. *The Message: The Bible in Contemporary Language.* Colorado Springs, CO: NavPress, 2002.

Wright, Nicholas Thomas. *Revelation for Everyone.* Louisville, KY: Westminster John Knox, 2011.

WOOD LAKE

Imagining, living, and telling the faith story.

WOOD LAKE IS THE FAITH STORY COMPANY.

It has told
■ the story of the seasons of the earth, the people of
God, and the place and purpose of faith in the world;
■ the story of the faith journey, from birth to death;
■ the story of Jesus and the churches that carry his
message.

Wood Lake has been telling stories for more than
35 years. During that time, it has given form and
substance to the words, songs, pictures, and ideas
of hundreds of storytellers.

Those stories have taken a multitude of forms –
parables, poems, drawings, prayers, epiphanies,
songs, books, paintings, hymns, curricula – all
driven by a common mission of serving those on
the faith journey.

Wood Lake Publishing Inc.

485 Beaver Lake Road
Kelowna, BC, Canada V4V 1S5
250.766.2778

www.woodlake.com